LISTENING TO THE BOYS

Meditations on Francisco de Zurbarán's
Jacob and His Twelve Sons

By David Pott

ISBN 978-1-5272-8249-0

Designed by Spark Design

Published by David Pott

Printed in Great Britain by Bell and Bain Ltd, Glasgow

Contents

Foreword

The power of art is a well-attested phenomenon, so it is no surprise that the link between the art of Zurbarán, currently displayed in a Palace which has been home to the Prince-Bishops of Durham for some 900 years, should be made at a time when the pictures belong, no longer to the proud prelates of yesteryear, but to the community of which they are a part.

God is a fiery sun, whose intensity of heat and light are unbearable to mortality – we shield our eyes from His Majesty. But God, in His love and mercy, gives us the gift of beauty – the light, as it were, of the moon – which is gentle, and pleads with us for attention, and yet is the same light, reflected, of the very sun itself.

How, then, can we respond to the moonlight of Jacob and the Patriarchs? We need to make this connection in our hearts, and David Pott's book is an invitation to do so. We need a guide to show how these paintings can play on the mind of those who choose to engage in this exercise, and we need to know the story – how excellently can the telling of a story help in this exercise! And in the telling of the story of these pictures, I perceive the guiding voice of David's wife, Pam, who is a supremely imaginative and humble story-teller.

I commend this book to all who sail on the journey of faith!

Jonathan Ruffer
Founder of The Auckland Project,
British City investor and art collector

INTRODUCTION

I think it is quite likely that my wife and I would not be living here near Bishop Auckland if Francisco de Zurbarán had not painted Jacob and His Twelve Sons in Seville 380 years ago!

In 2015 we were living on the Isle of Arran and we knew it was time to move, but where to? When we visited friends in Bishop Auckland, we soon became interested to hear about plans that were underway to transform Bishop Auckland into a visitor destination. The fact that all this had started through a campaign to keep a set of paintings by Zurbarán at Auckland Castle was something else that intrigued me.

Although my great great grandfather Laslett Pott was a distinguished Victorian history painter who exhibited 43 works at the Royal Academy, I have never been able to draw or paint anything - I dread a game of Pictionary! But when I was about seventeen, I went to an exhibition of works by the French Romantic artist Delacroix at the Scottish National Gallery in Edinburgh. His name sounded like the crack of a whip and his paintings were so full of colour and high drama. That began a lifetime of enjoyment finding out about different artists and their work.

Roll on fifty years and more and I entered the Long Dining Room at Auckland Castle and met Jacob and his Twelve Sons for the first time in the summer of 2015. Since that time, I have enjoyed some more face to face encounters at the castle and have also spent time finding out more about the paintings and their remarkable story.

I am on an unfinished journey and this little book of reflections and meditations is an opportunity to share what I have learnt along the way so far. For a first class introduction to the paintings, I highly recommend Robert McManners' excellent book *Zurbaráns at Auckland Castle* published by Gemini Productions. My very brief introduction here includes the amazing story of how they came to Auckland Castle and something about the unity and diversity in the set of portraits. The main substance of the book follows with meditations on each of the thirteen paintings. Zurbarán painted from a Christian perspective which I share, but, with the difference in time and place, we would not be wearing exactly the same pair of glasses! I hope that the meditations will, however, be accessible and relevant, whatever your own perspective might be.

The title Listening to the Boys is used for two reasons. Firstly, it is because the paintings are sometimes affectionately known as 'the boys', or even by Lydia Nicholson, one of the volunteer guides, as 'my boys'! That's a strong indication of just how special these paintings are for Bishop Auckland. Secondly, it is an aid to the intention that you, as a reader, should be an active reader, listening to what each of 'the boys' has to say to you. This is why there is space after each meditation for you to record your own reflections.

ABOUT ZURBARÁN HIMSELF

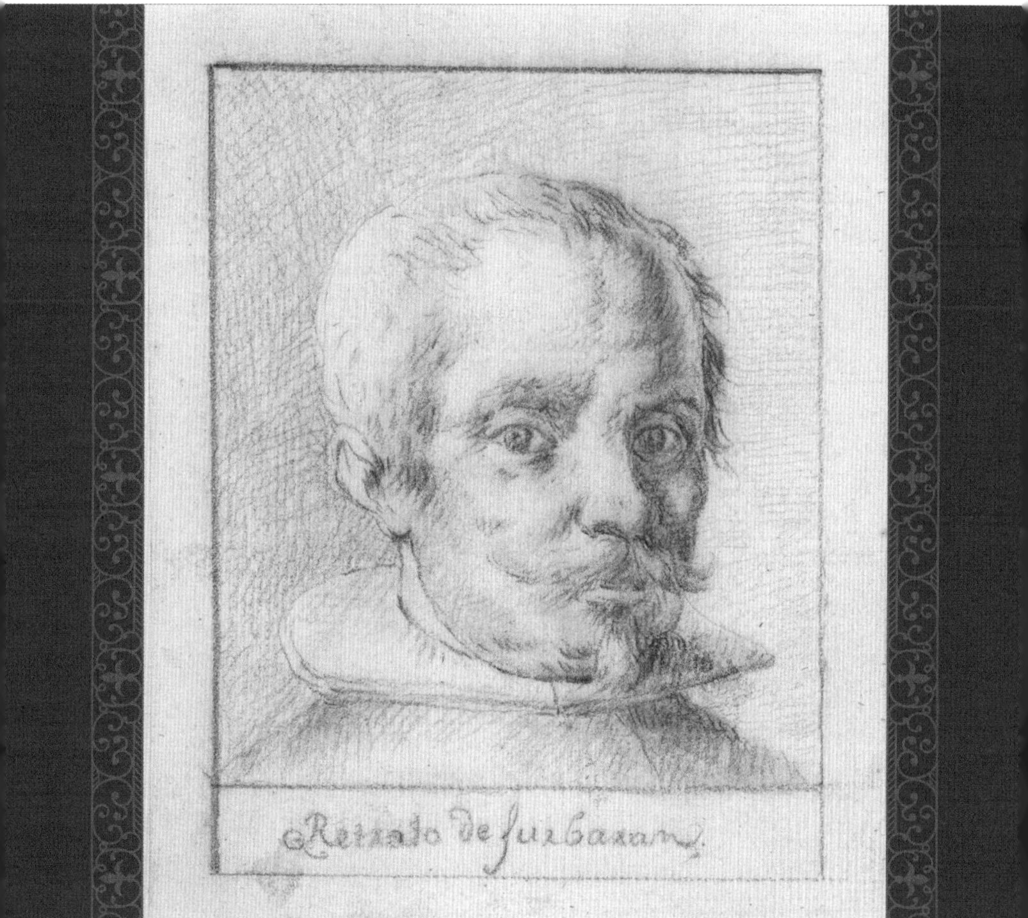

Portrait of Francisco de Zurbarán by Francisco de Goya, c.1798, The Louvre, Paris. Goya based his sketch on a portrait which is now lost.

Francisco de Zurbarán was born in 1598 in a little village called Fuente de Cantos in Extremadura in south west Spain. Even as a little child he started to draw very good village scenes in charcoal, so when he was 16, his father sent him to be an apprentice for three years to an experienced artist in the city of Seville. After he was apprenticed at the age of 19, he married María Paet, who was nine years older than him. He also set up his studio in the town of Llerena.

Over the next twenty years or so, Zurbarán became a very well known painter indeed. But while things were going well in his career, his family life was difficult. His first wife Maria died in 1624 while giving birth to their third child. The next year he married a wealthy widow called Beatriz de Morales.

He was asked to do many paintings for clients in Seville and quite often he was commuting from Llerena to Seville and that was a two day journey each way! Eventually the town council persuaded him to move his workshop to the city. He moved there with his family as well as eight servants in 1629.

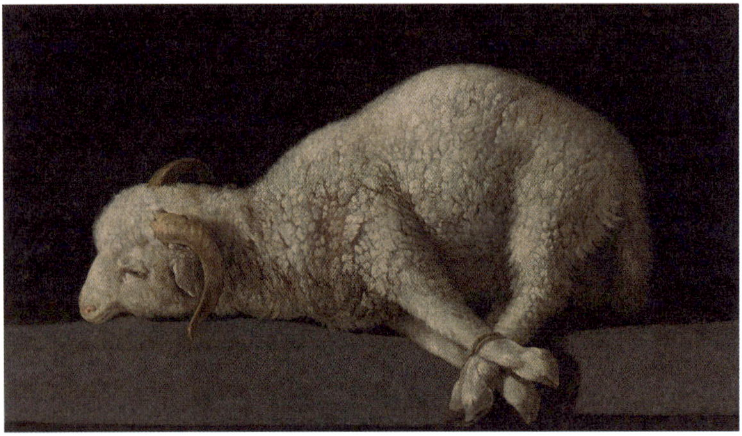

Agnus Dei (The Lamb of God)

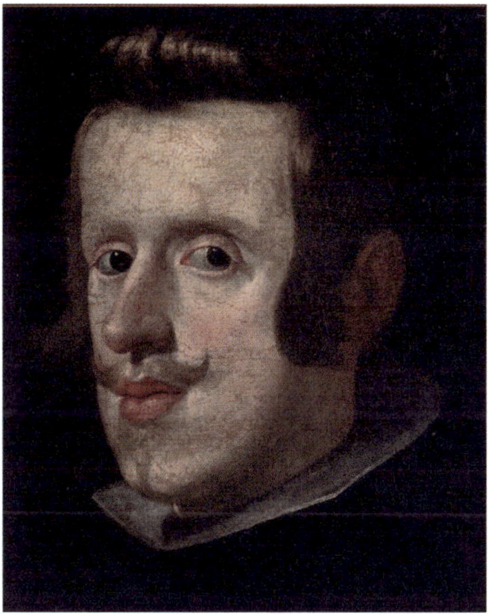

Portrait of King Philip IV of Spain, before 1650, by Francisco de Zurbarán, Slovak National Gallery - Betliar Museum

Zurbarán was very well known for his skill in using light and darkness in his paintings and for an amazing attention to fine detail. This is very clearly seen in his famous painting of the bound lamb called Agnus Dei.

Zurbarán's great skill as an artist led to his appointment as painter to King Philip IV. This is his portrait of the king. There is a story that the king once laid his hand on Zurbarán's shoulder and said, "Painter to the king, king of painters".

In 1639 his second wife Beatriz died and after that time his paintings became less popular in Spain. Seville was the main trading port for all the Spanish colonies in South America and it was at this time that Zurbarán started to paint for clients there especially in Lima and Buenos Aires. In 1644, he married for a third time to another widow called Leonor de Tordera and they had four children. In order to make ends meet, he even sold some paints and brushes to artists in South America as well as some Flemish paintings. It was during this difficult decade of his life that Zurbarán painted our special Jacob and his Twelve Sons series.

A STORY OF RECONCILIATION AND REGENERATION

At the time that Zurbarán executed these paintings in the 1640s, the Jews were experiencing persecution in Spain at the hands of the Inquisition. Many 'conversos' (Jews who had officially converted to Roman Catholicism) had remained after the expulsion of the Jews from Spain in 1492, but they were constantly being watched for signs of reverting to Jewish practices.

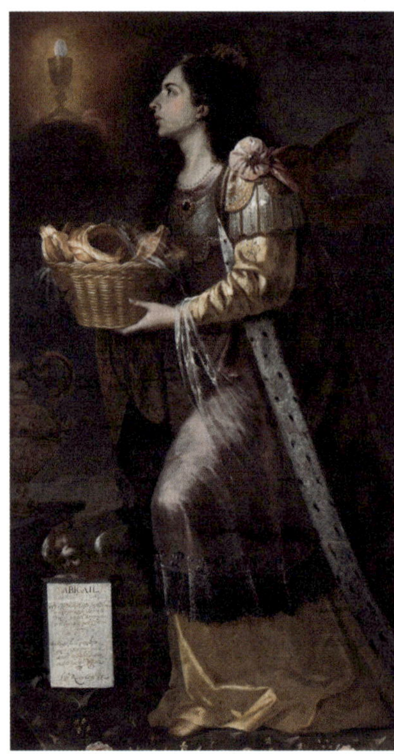

Abigail, Circle of Zurbarán

Perhaps it was this intense suspicion of Judaism which was a reason for the paucity of paintings of Old Testament subjects in Spanish art. On the rare occasions when Old Testament subjects were chosen, they were allegorical in nature and pointing forward to the New Testament. There is an example of this from the School of Zurbarán in a painting of Abigail. The story is told in 1 Samuel 25, where Abigail intercepts David and his men who are on their way to deal with her husband Nabal after he had insulted David. She brought gifts for David which included two hundred loaves of bread and two skins of wine, so this painting, with the mystic chalice in the background, strongly alludes to Christ and the Eucharist.

With regard to the subject of Jacob and his sons, there is no record of a commission for the subject ever being ordered for use in Spain itself. However there was a demand in Latin America, because at that time it was widely held that the indigenous people of South America were descendants of the lost tribes of Israel. This theory was originally promoted by Bartholeme de Las Casas (1484-1566) who became the champion of the Native American Indians, devoting his lifetime to improving their conditions. Las Casas wrote: "These Indians can bring near the redemption. If we treat them humanely in this world and convert them to Christianity, we are preparing for the redemption of the Western world in the messianic era. Their conversion is apt indeed, as I am convinced the Indians originate in Ancient Israel. Indeed, I can bring proofs from the Bible that they are of the Lost Tribes".

The theory continued to gain momentum in the seventeenth century. A text that was sometimes cited was 2 Esdras 13:41 in the Apocrypha which stated that the tribes fled "to a more distant region, where no human beings had ever lived". As an aid to missionary endeavours to the indigenous peoples of Latin America, the theme of Jacob and his sons became a very popular one in the visual arts. This included the creation of effigies of Jacob and his sons being carried in religious processions in cities like Lima. By the time Zurbarán and his team had begun painting the Auckland Castle series, he had already had two commissions of the same subject which are now in Lima, Peru and Puebla in Mexico.

It is generally thought most likely that the series was also destined for South America, but there is no record of the provenance of these paintings until the 1720s. The missing eighty years provide ample opportunity for speculation! One is the suggestion that the paintings may have been discovered on board a Spanish vessel captured by the British. When the series was on display in Jerusalem in 2018, a reviewer suggested that Jewish pirates who were in league with the British could be another possibility. The Jewish pirates of the Caribbean were formed by Jews who had fled persecution in Spain and who took every opportunity to take revenge on the Spanish when opportunity arose. Could the high quality of the paintings have meant that a wealthy Spaniard or indeed a Jewish *converso* intervened with a higher price? Could they have originally gone to Latin America, but then returned for some unknown reason? In all probability we will never know what happened to the paintings in those missing years. At all events, in 1722 the paintings were sold by Sir William Chapman (most probably to pay off South Sea Bubble debts) to a Jewish banker in London called James Mendez.

In 1756, twelve of the thirteen paintings were purchased for £124 from the estate of Mendez (who had died in 1749) by Richard Trevor who was the Bishop of Durham. The painting of Benjamin was sold separately, but Bishop Trevor commissioned Arthur Pond to paint a copy so that he could complete the set. Although we do not have conclusive proof of this, it is very likely that Bishop Trevor had a very clear motivation for buying the paintings. He was a strong supporter of The Jewish Naturalisation Bill which was passed in 1753, but after riots and much opposition, the bill was quickly repealed. The intensity of anti-Semitism in England at this time is clearly shown in the satirical print from 1753. The text at the bottom begins and ends as follows: "Gods word declares the Jews a Vagrant race ... And then (without them) you will a Happier Canaan find". St Paul's Cathedral is in the background as it was rumoured that the Jews planned to turn it into a synagogue. There is a circumcision knife lying beside the priestly garment because it was said that all English males would be circumcised if the Jews were given more rights.

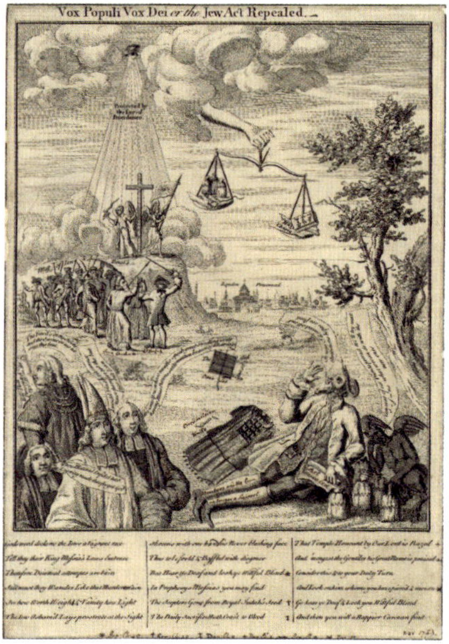

Vox Populi Vox Dei or the Jew Act Repealed

It seems likely then that Bishop Trevor bought the paintings as an act of reconciliation and to express his strong support of Jewish naturalisation rights. Bishop Trevor then proceeded to rebuild the Long Dining Room at the castle to enable the paintings to be displayed to full advantage to all his guests. It has rightly been described by Robert McManners as "a gallery of conscience".

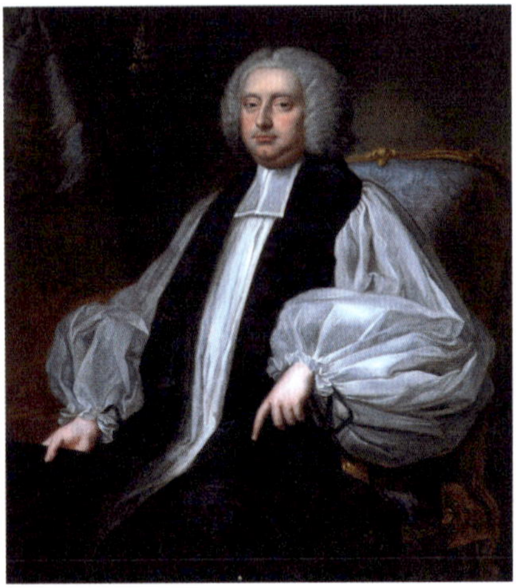

Richard Trevor, Bishop of Durham, 1756 by Thomas Hudson (1701-1779)

Another reason for Bishop Trevor buying Jacob and His Twelve Sons is that it was part of his plan to bring together paintings in the castle which emphasised the foundations of the faith and of the church. When visitors came through the Great Room they would encounter paintings of the twelve apostles by an unknown Spanish artist. To these he added paintings of the four evangelists by the Flemish artist Artus Wolfaerts and finally a painting of the Four Fathers of the Latin Church by Abraham Bloemaert from Utrecht in Holland. The last purchase is a particularly interesting one as the subject matter with St Augustine, St Jerome, St Ambrose and St Gregory discussing the doctrine of transubstantiation was considered a very Catholic subject. Perhaps this is further evidence of Bishop Trevor's broad mindedness and spirit of reconciliation in an age of intolerance. He is also known to have had good relationships with dissenters. We can easily imagine Bishop Trevor unpacking the symbolic significance of the two twelves followed by the two fours to his guests at the castle!

The apostles are no longer at Auckland Castle, but some can be seen at Durham Castle. The four evangelists can still be seen in the Long Dining Room with Jacob and his Twelve Sons, but the Four Fathers by Bloemart was sold by the

Church Commissioners in 1972 and is now at the Catherijneconvent in Utrecht. Auckland Castle has recently purchased a painting of the same subject by Jacob Jordaens who lived all his life in Antwerp.

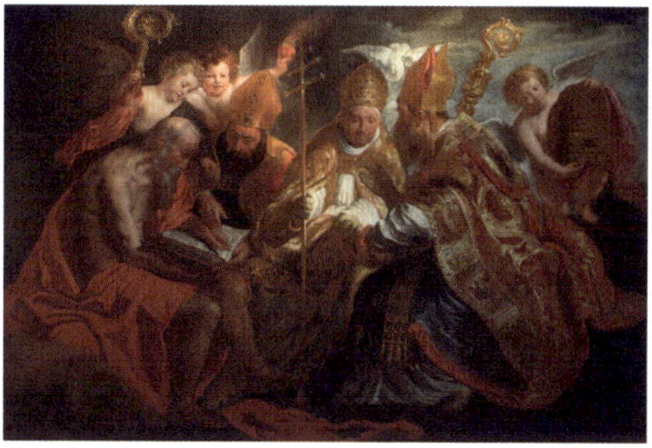

The Four Fathers of the Latin Church by Jacob Jordaens (1593-1678)

In 2001, the Church Commissioners voted to sell the paintings. The likelihood of the paintings leaving the castle was very bad news for Bishop Auckland, which had fallen on hard times following the closure of the coal mines in the second half of the twentieth century. Fortunately in 2011, the paintings, along with the castle, were bought for £15million by the Christian philanthropist Jonathan Ruffer, who is a keen collector of Spanish Art. He and his wife Jane set up The Auckland Project and have devoted their lives to the regeneration of Bishop Auckland as a visitor destination. It is amazing to reflect that Zurbarán's paintings, with their special subject matter and extraordinary history, have now become the means of initiating the spiritual, social and economic regeneration of Bishop Auckland and the surrounding area.

THE ZURBARÁNS COME TO TOWN

On Christmas Eve 2019, 13 life-size collage models based on Jacob and His Twelve Sons were paraded, along with other models for a nativity scene, through the streets of Bishop Auckland.

As we have seen, there were parades in the seventeenth century with models of Jacob and his sons in Lima, Peru and Puebla in Mexico. They also occurred in Seville. Our parade would have been culturally and visually a very different affair from those parades in Spain and Latin America, but it is intriguing to think that this might have been the first town parade of Jacob and his sons for nigh on four hundred years!

The context of this event was an initiative called Bishop Auckland Advent Windows which is organised by the Bishop Auckland Town Team. The format is that of a giant advent calendar, whereby each day between December 1st and 24th, a different shop opens up a window on a Christmas theme. Every shop is in partnership with a school or other community group which designs the window. In 2019, we engaged a local artist, Laura Brenchley, to inspire and lead the schools and community groups to make 24 life-size models. This included making Jacob and his sons who were all cast as shepherds, wise men and other characters to include in what we called our alterNativity scene.

One of the reasons for making the models was that we believed that it was important for the people of Bishop Auckland to get to know the amazing Zurbarán paintings better and understand that they belong to the town. The project was a means of reinterpreting them and enabling them to come out of their confinement in the castle and enter into the town!

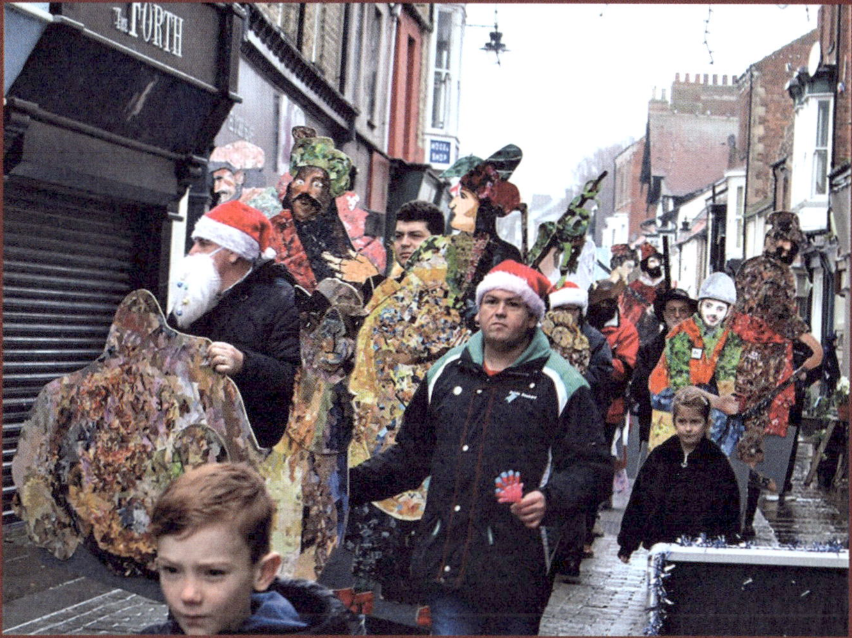

Parade with models in Bishop Auckland

THE PAINTINGS THEMSELVES – UNITY AND DIVERSITY

These paintings relate to the occasion recorded in Genesis 49 when Jacob, who was about to die, called his sons and said: "Gather round so that I can tell you what will happen to you in days to come. Assemble and listen, sons of Jacob, listen to your father Israel". Indeed the set of paintings is like a gathering still: Jacob and his sons are preserved for all time and we, as viewers, are invited to listen and perceive what the paintings have to say to us in our own time.

What these paintings have to say is not always easy listening. This chapter in Genesis is often headed as "Jacob blesses his sons", but it is more accurate to say that he prophesies over his sons. In some cases Jacob appears to speak more about the destiny of the tribe rather than that of the individual.

The paintings have a compelling power and it almost seems as if the figures could step out towards you from the frames. Their larger than life size is accentuated by the low landscapes and the vast cloudy skies. There are some other features that are common to all the paintings and help to give a sense of unity. These include the stone blocks in the foreground corners where the sons are all numbered and named and also in each of the paintings light is coming in from the left, creating a consistent pattern of light and shade throughout the set.

Within this unified context, Zurbarán's imaginative genius is displayed in the way that each portrait is utterly unique. The extraordinary variety of clothing on display is what first draws one's attention. It is like a procession of people in fancy dress and indeed some have suspected that Zurbarán may have been influenced by the tradition of exotic processions at significant religious festivals in Spain. Another influence may have come from his father, who was a haberdasher. Perhaps the paintings were a means of advertising his wares! It is well worth taking time to compare specific items like headgear or footwear. Notice too the great variety of postures and gestures and unusually three of the portraits are from the back.

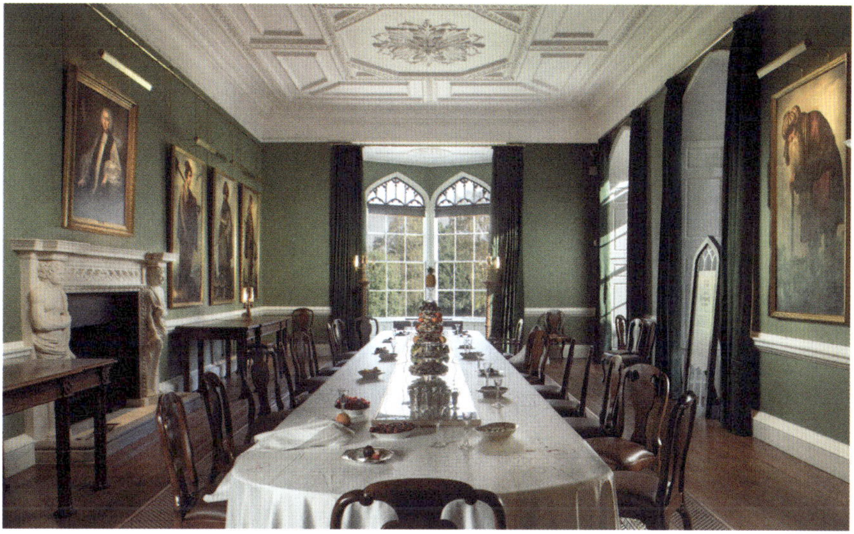

The Long Dining Room at Auckland Castle, which has been dressed for one of Bishop Trevor's dinner parties. This has been the home of the paintings for over 260 years.

There are no halos here because Zurbarán paints the brothers in all their humanity. In a review of the paintings, the Jewish American writer Menachem Wecker pointed out that in most previous paintings of the twelve sons, the mothers would not have been able to distinguish between them! But Zurbarán has understood perfectly that in the Bible, "even the most exalted figures are depicted neither as saints nor as angels but as all-too-fallible human beings. There are good and bad parents, good and bad sibling relationships, praiseworthy and dishonourable actions. If his predecessors had almost universally avoided the darker moral areas in order to project images of unsullied piety, Zurbarán—who in this respect shares a sensibility with his towering Dutch contemporary Rembrandt—preserves and enlivens the tensions". *

The paintings are a reminder that God's purposes in this world often unfold through groups of unlikely people. In this regard, we have already noted that as well as buying the Zurburáns, Bishop Trevor also bought a set of the twelve apostles. It is likely that Zurbarán as well as Bishop Trevor had in mind the concept of Jacob and his sons as types of Christ and the twelve apostles. Indeed Edward Payne writing in the catalogue for the Frick Collection exhibition writes: "Contemporary viewers would have understood the paintings in allegorical terms, as the Blessings of Jacob reveal God's plan for the salvation of the world through the death and resurrection of his son, Jesus Christ". **

** From review in MOSAIC Magazine March 2018*

*** See page 12 of exhibition catalogue: Zurbarán: Jacob and His Twelve Sons, Paintings from Auckland Castle. Dec 2017*

LOOKING, LISTENING, LEARNING...

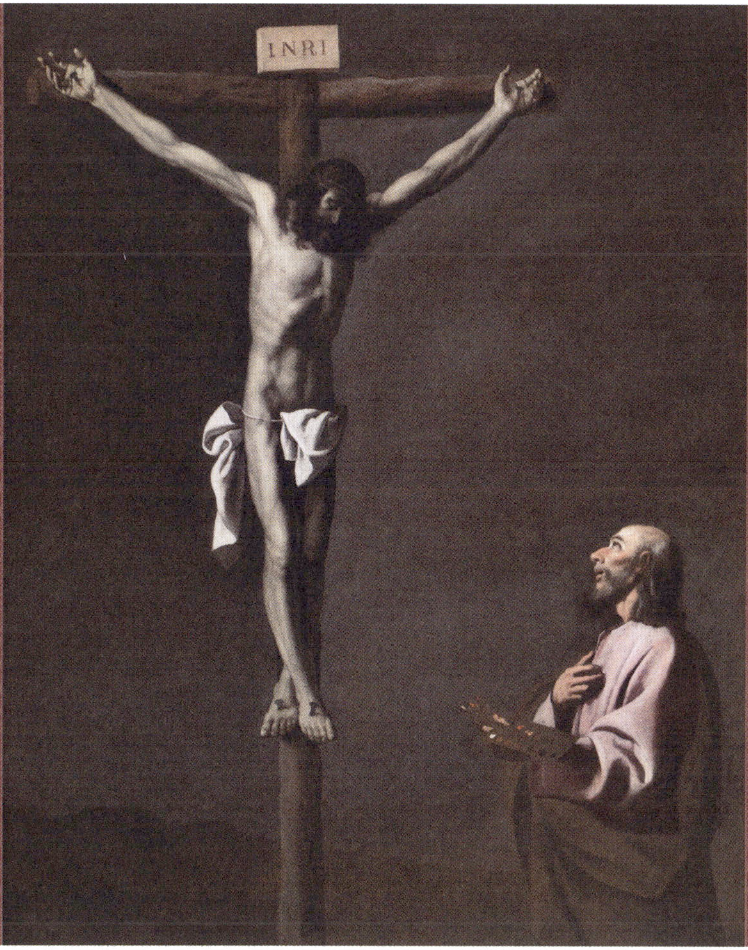

In this painting of The Crucified Christ with a Painter, it is thought that the painter is Zurbarán himself. Does this add weight to the idea that Zurbarán is often pointing to Christ in the Jacob and sons series?

Imagine that, just as Jacob gathered his sons together to hear these prophecies, you also are invited to join the gathering. Look and listen expectantly and see what the paintings have to say to you. It may be that you are drawn to a character who attracts you or, alternatively, it may be one you want to question or debate with. Hopefully this will lead to fruitful meditation. There are comments to help you under each of the reproductions, but hopefully you will receive fresh insights for yourself.

As you look at these famous paintings, it would also be good to bear in mind the following things...

- Zurbarán was a storyteller as well as a painter. Frequently these paintings have a direct or indirect reference to a story elsewhere in the Bible. I have suggested what some of those stories might be, but you may find others as you reflect on the paintings.
- The number twelve is very significant in the Bible and in particular speaks of foundations. Here is a section from Revelation 21:12-14 about the New Jerusalem which highlights this:
  "It had a large, high wall with twelve gates. Twelve angels were at the gates, and ***the names of the twelve tribes of Israel were written on the gates****. There were three gates on the east, three gates on the north, three gates on the south, and three gates on the west. The wall of the city had twelve foundations, and the twelve names of the twelve apostles of the Lamb were written on them".*
  Do the paintings speak about any values that are foundational for society?

- We have seen that Jacob's blessings are more accurately described as prophecies. It seems that Zurbarán catches this spirit of prophecy and that the paintings have a power to continue to speak in our own time.
- After you have spent some time looking at a painting, you may like to imagine the character stepping out of the frame to have a conversation with you! What might they like to ask you and what would you like to ask them? How might they answer? Use the blank space after each meditation to record what you hear.

I would like to share here an example of someone who 'listened' to what one of the paintings (Joseph) had to say to him:

"My encounter with this painting left me with a profound sense of healing and liberation. I knew the story: after his brothers had betrayed Joseph, they came back to him seeking grain during a time of famine. I imagined I was one of these brothers, guilty of the same pettiness and in need of a similar forgiveness. My eyes at first rested on the folded petitions in Joseph's right hand, which became my petitions. His pointed index finger then drew my attention to the slender rod in his left, a symbol of his authority to judge, but also of his power to grant requests. I looked up to his eyes and was met with warmth and exceeding mercy: Zurbarán's Joseph mirrors the image of Christ Pantocrator, the all-powerful judge of humanity, popular in Orthodox Churches, whose stern yet tender gaze sustains the entire world. The portrait thus becomes an icon, a visible assurance of God's presence, before which it is impossible to feel judged in any way — except positively".

This was written by Griffin Oleynick in *Commonweal Magazine* of March 3rd 2018.

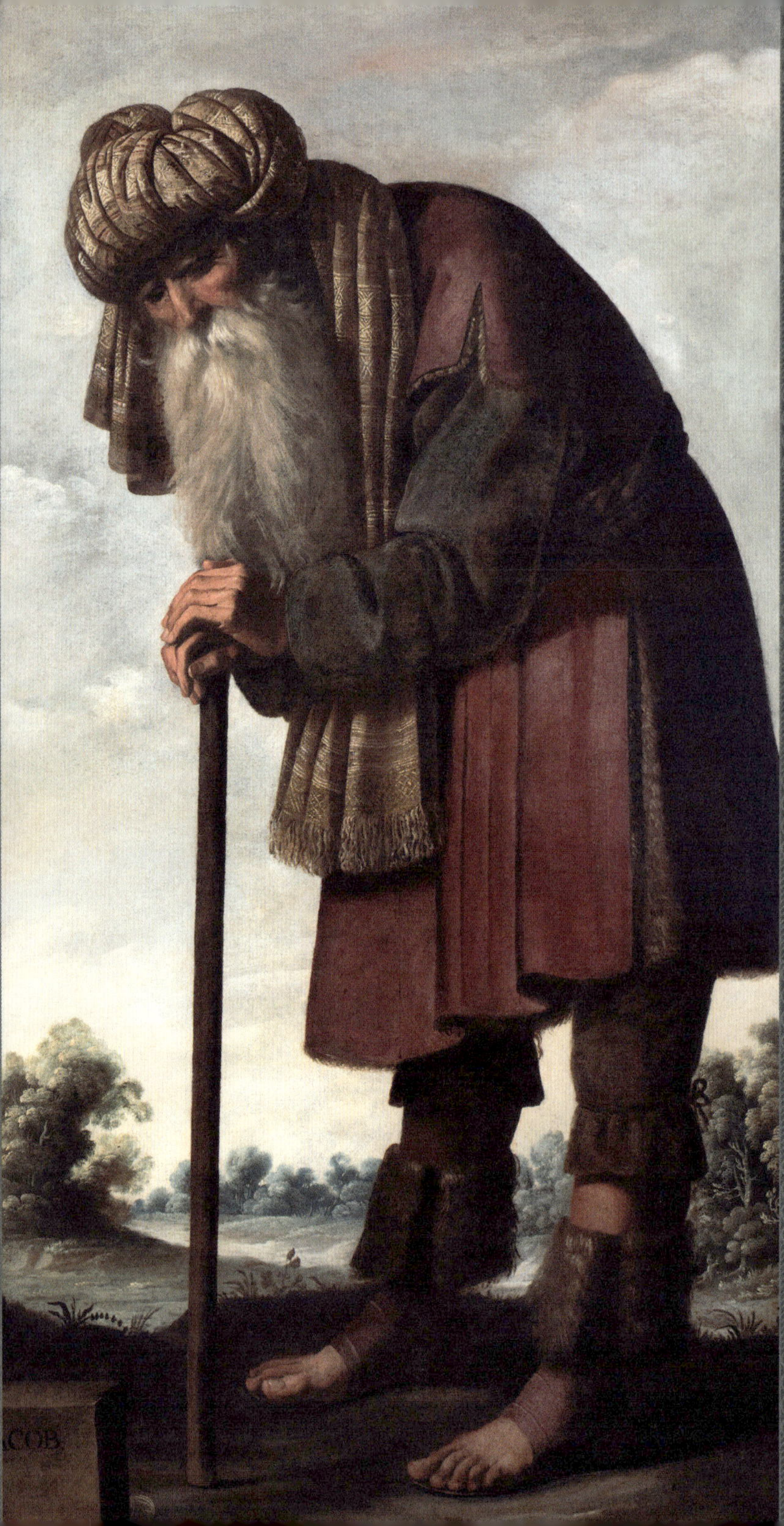
ACOB.

JACOB THE WORSHIPPER

Although Jacob is very close to the end of his life, Zurbarán has painted him in a paradoxical manner so that as well as being frail, Jacob is solid and substantial. We can feel the weight of his body with the hands pressed down on his staff. The downward vertical lines of his scarf, his magnificent white beard and his cloak add to the sense that here is someone bringing down some weighty revelations from above.

What does the sad expression on Jacob's face suggest to you?

Is he reflecting on his past life? When he met with Pharaoh, he described his 130 years as being *"few and difficult and they do not equal the years of the pilgrimage of my fathers".* (Genesis 47:9). Was Jacob remembering troubling episodes in his life such as when he stole the birthright from his hairy brother Esau by disguising himself with animal skins, an incident which is cleverly alluded to in the furry ankle cuffs Zurbarán has included? No doubt at this moment, Jacob would also be feeling the weight of responsibility in his final task of bringing these sometimes uncomfortable prophecies to his sons.

However Zurbarán may also have been wanting to convey something else through the particular posture of Jacob in this painting. In the list of the heroes of faith in Hebrews 11:21 we read: *"By faith, Jacob when he was dying, blessed each of Joseph's sons, and worshipped as he leaned on the top of his staff".* Joseph's two sons, Ephraim and Manasseh, were blessed shortly before Jacob called together his own sons to prophesy over them. Zurbarán is again portraying something paradoxical - certainly the sorrows and regrets of Jacob's life are being shown, but the major theme is that of worship. Jacob is not just bowed down by the weight of his years and his troubles, but is also bowing down in humility and reverential worship in the spirit of Psalm 95:6 *"Come let us bow down in worship".* When we think of worship in the English language, we tend to be influenced over much by the old English origin of the word as ***worth**-ship.* However, in the original Hebrew and Greek words used in the Bible, there is a strong physicality in the meaning of the word which is 'to bow down or prostrate yourself.'

Meditation Suggestions

- If Jacob could speak out of the painting, perhaps these are the sort of words he would say to us: "If you feel bowed down by the troubles of this world, bow down and worship my God, the God of Jacob. Though I have often failed him, He has always been faithful and led me throughout this hard pilgrimage and somehow, in spite of me, His good purposes have come to pass through my life". Use these thoughts as a basis for reflecting on situations in your own life.
- What does this painting suggest to you about the meaning of worship?
- What does Zurbarán convey about old age in the painting?

Listening to Jacob

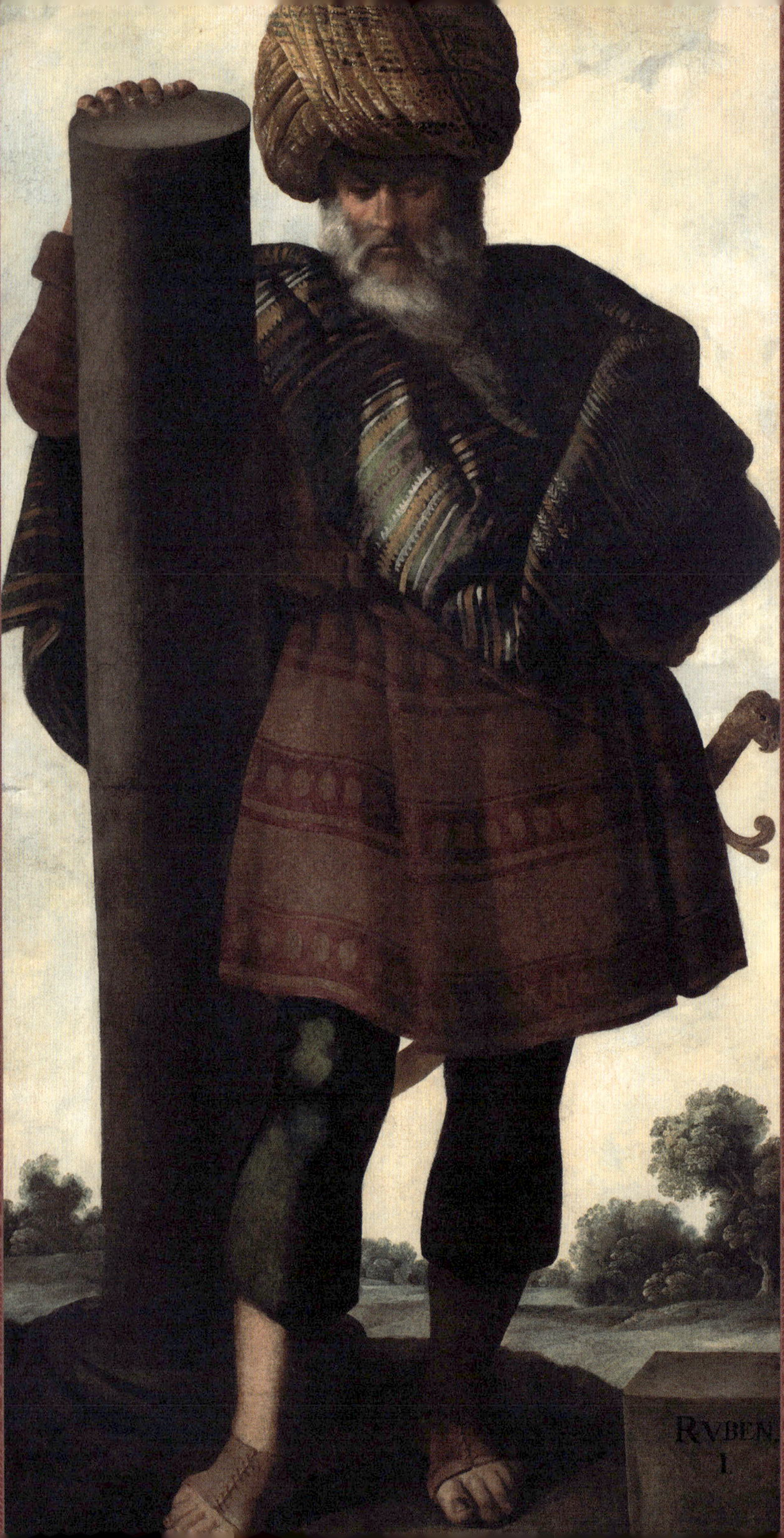
RVBEN
I.

REUBEN THE UNSTABLE

'Reuben, you are my firstborn,
my might, the first sign of my strength,
excelling in honour, excelling in power.
Turbulent as the waters, you will no longer excel,
for you went up onto your father's bed,
onto my couch and defiled it.'

Genesis 49:3,4

The name Reuben in Hebrew means 'Behold, a son' and in the first half of the prophecy it seems that Jacob is taking pride in his firstborn. This suddenly turns in the second half, where Jacob refers to an incident mentioned in Genesis 35:22, which records Reuben sleeping with Bilhah, Jacob's concubine.

Zurbarán has managed to convey something of the ambiguity in his portrait. Reuben is imposing and dominant with his high turban and impressive cloak and a huge sword at his side. However there is something evasive in his expression, perhaps suggestive of guilt. The very realistic parrot head at the top of Reuben's sword could almost be saying, "I could tell you a thing or two about this guy!".

Apart from Reuben himself, the most prominent feature is the pillar. Pillars are symbols of strength and stability. This is the exact opposite of the water in the second half of the prophesy which is described as "unstable" in the Authorised Version. The fact that he rests his right hand on the pillar suggests that the God given destiny for Reuben is to let go of his instability and instead become a pillar of society.

Meditation Suggestions

- The giving of names was always very significant in Hebrew culture. Reuben's name meaning 'Behold, a son', calls to mind the famous prophecy in Isaiah 7:14 "Behold a virgin will conceive and bear a son and will call his name Immanuel". This was fulfilled when Jesus Christ was born and like Reuben, he too was the first born. What does your name mean? Is that meaning significant for you?
- Psalm 148:12 reads: "Our sons in their youth will be like well-nurtured plants, and our daughters will be like pillars carved to adorn a palace". What do you think are key factors in bringing up children who will become pillars in society?

Listening to Reuben

SIMEON THE VIOLENT MAN

'Simeon and Levi are brothers –
their swords are weapons of violence.
Let me not enter their council,
let me not join their assembly,
for they have killed men in their anger
and hamstrung oxen as they pleased.
Cursed be their anger, so fierce,
and their fury, so cruel!
I will scatter them in Jacob
and disperse them in Israel.'

Genesis 49:5-7

This is the hardest prophecy of all and it is given to Simeon and Levi together but we will focus on Simeon first.

Jacob is referring to the occasion recorded in Genesis 34 when Simeon and Levi took vicious revenge after their sister Dinah had been raped by Shechem. Jacob had been seeking some sort of reconciliation with Shechem's father Hamor, which involved all the men of the town agreeing to being circumcised in exchange for Shechem being allowed to marry Dinah. Soon after the men had been circumcised, Simeon

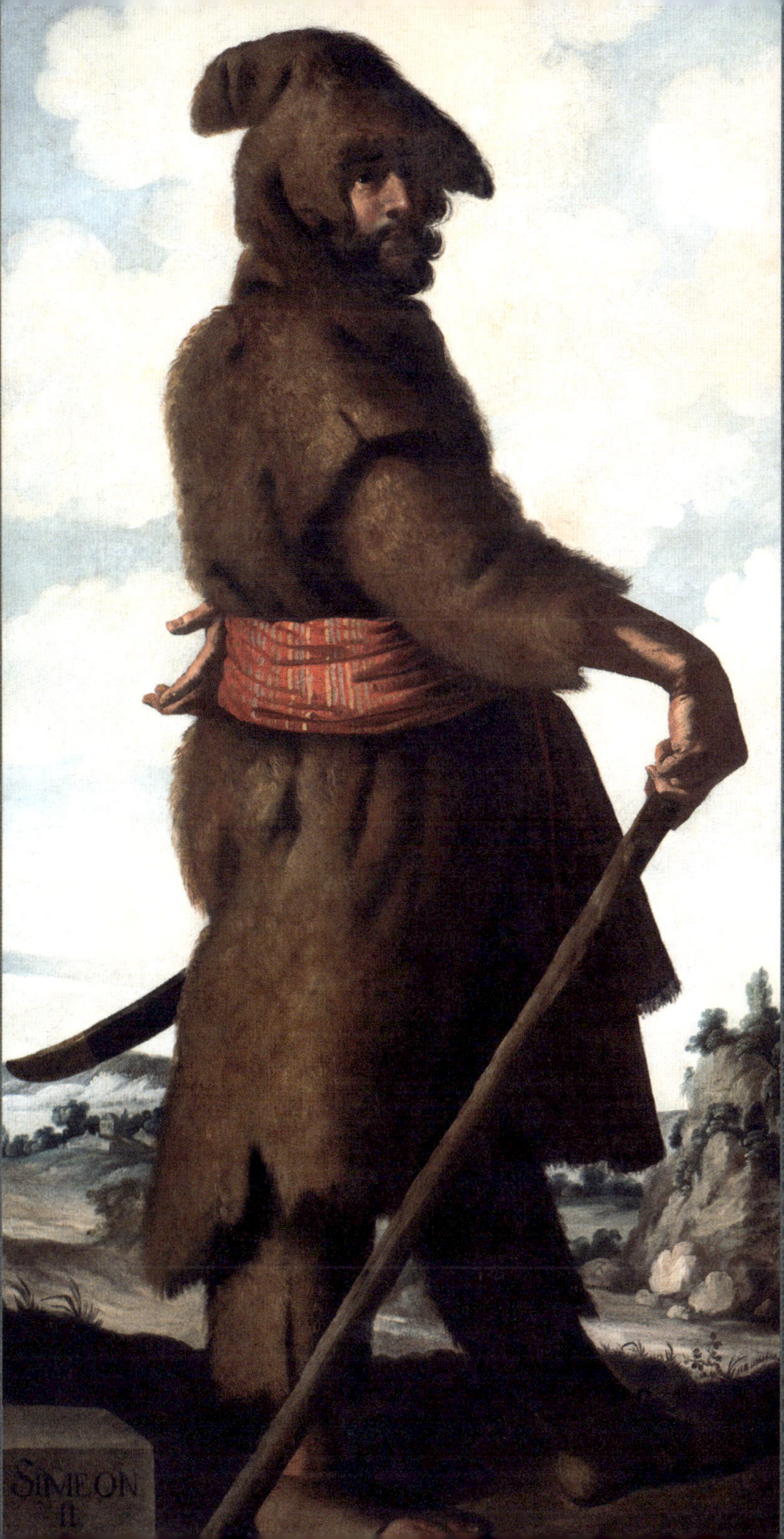
SIMEON
II.

and Levi came and slaughtered them all and carried off their women and children.

Significantly Jacob said to Simeon and Levi, "You have brought trouble on me by making me obnoxious to the Canaanites and Perizzites". Violence begets violence and the Israelites were destined to be frequently at war with the Canaanites and Perizzites.

Zurbarán painted Simeon as a vagabond in rough animal skins including a threatening hoodie. He has a sword at his side and a wooden club.

Meditation Suggestions

- Simeon's name means 'listening' and this is something important as you view this painting. You might want to move hurriedly on, but listen to hear the message of this painting regarding the futility of violence.
- Reflect on Jesus who was the Prince of Peace, consistently rejecting violence and saying those radical words, *"Love your enemies and pray for those who persecute you".* (Matthew 5:44)
- There was another person in scripture who had the name Simeon. He was an elderly man, who all his life had been listening and waiting attentively for the coming of the Messiah. One day as he was listening, he heard the voice of the Holy Spirit prompting him to go to the Temple. There he found that infant Messiah Jesus with Mary and Joseph. Simeon prophesied that He would be a light to the nations.

Listening to Simeon

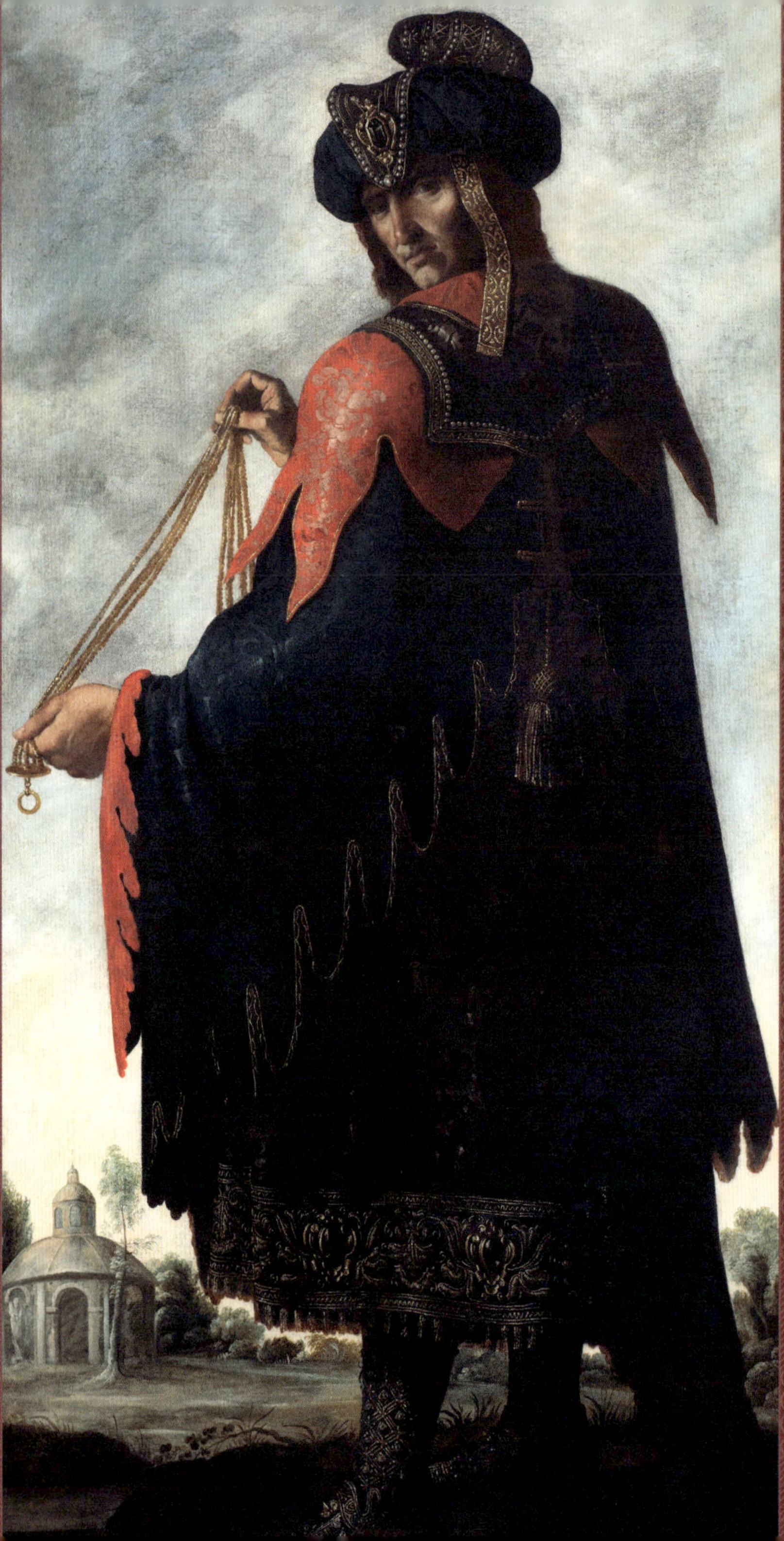

LEVI THE PRIEST

Zurbarán painted Levi in a completely different way from Simeon and it seems that he almost certainly drew more of his inspiration from the blessing of Moses on the tribe of Levi and in particular these words:

'He teaches your precepts to Jacob
and your law to Israel.
He offers incense before you
and whole burnt offerings on your altar.
Bless all his skills, Lord,
and be pleased with the work of his hands.'

Deuteronomy 33:10,11

One particular aspect of Jacob's prophecy which was clearly fulfilled in Levi's case was *"I will scatter them in Jacob and disperse them in Israel"*. The tribe had no land inheritance in Israel and lived amongst all the other tribes. Incidentally the prophecy was also fulfilled in Simeon's case as that tribe was located at the southern margins of Israel and was to some extent incorporated within Judah.

In the painting, Levi is looking back over his shoulder and, significantly, carries an incense burner in his hands. The task of this tribe of priests is to minister directly to God through the regular offering of the sacrifices in the temple which is illustrated in the background. They are also commissioned to ensure that the people are constantly taught God's law. The name Levi means 'joined' and that name is suggestive of their role in connecting the people to God.

However Zurbarán also hints at something rather sinister. In all his finery, Levi looks down at us from a position of spiritual arrogance and superiority. Has he got something to hide? He is a reminder that a position of spiritual power is full of temptations to misuse that power which can lead to sexual and other kinds of abuse and violence. Zurbarán would have been all too aware of this at a time when the Spanish Inquisition was so actively persecuting the Jews.

Meditation Suggestions

- Perhaps this is a time to remember the Pope and other leaders who have the challenging task of dealing with those who abuse power in their own churches.
- Levi was the name of one of the twelve apostles who was also called Matthew. He lived up to the meaning of his name by leaving behind his job as a tax collector and joining the company of those who followed Jesus. As you look at this painting of the first Levi, imagine the rich and well dressed Levi Matthew and reflect on how different a portrait of him might look after a year or two on the road with Jesus!

Listening to Levi

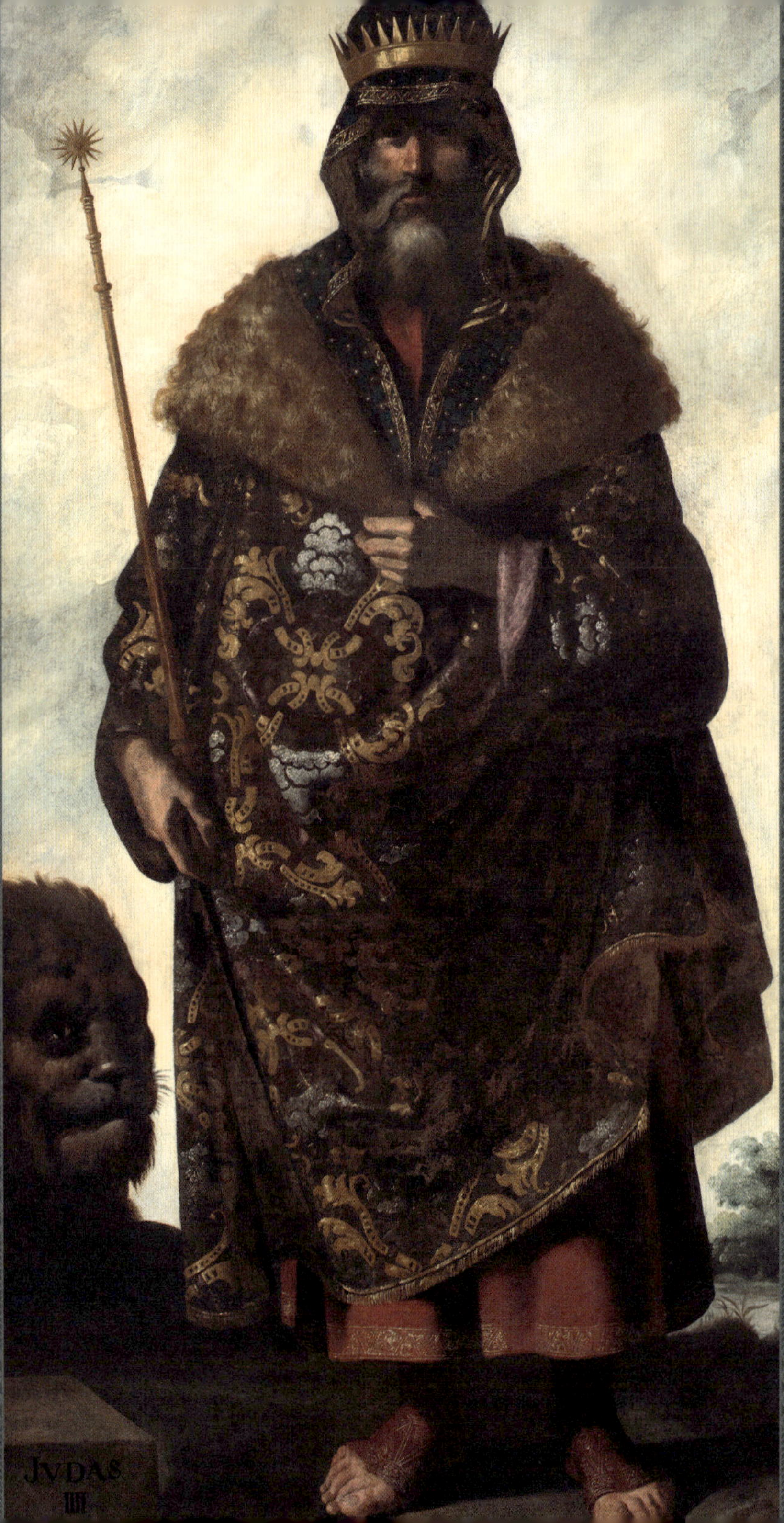
JVDAS
IIII

JUDAH THE KING

'Judah, your brothers will praise you;
your hand will be on the neck of your enemies;
your father's sons will bow down to you.
You are a lion's cub, Judah;
you return from the prey, my son.
Like a lion he crouches and lies down,
like a lioness – who dares to rouse him?
The sceptre will not depart from Judah,
nor the ruler's staff from between his feet,
until he to whom it belongs shall come
and the obedience of the nations shall be his.
He will tether his donkey to a vine,
his colt to the choicest branch;
he will wash his garments in wine,
his robes in the blood of grapes.
His eyes will be darker than wine,
his teeth whiter than milk.'

Genesis 49:8-12

Judah is the unmistakable crowned king in royal robes looking out confidently from this painting and holding the royal sun-crowned sceptre. At his feet is the curious face of a lion. It is quite likely that Zurbarán had never seen a lion, but he also may have deliberately given him human features reflecting the closeness of the animal/human metaphor.

This prophecy reaches much further into the future beyond the destiny of the tribe to the true Lion of Judah in Jesus Christ. In Revelation 5:5 Jesus is described as *"the Lion of the tribe of Judah and the root of Jesse"*. The prophecy indicates that Jesus Christ, a descendent of the tribe of Judah, is the one to whom all the nations will come. Mention of the donkey/colt and his robes washed in the blood of grapes surely points to Christ's Passion. Is there a hint of the colour of a rich wine on Judah's robes?

Meditation Suggestions

- As you look at this painting think about whether this image of Judah is similar or dissimilar to how you imagine Christ as King. Jesus came to establish not a political entity, but rather the Kingdom of God, a multi-ethnic worldwide family under the good rule of the Lion of Judah.
- Judah's name means 'praise' which is directly referred to in the first line of the prophecy. Meditate on the word praise and what it means for you.

Listening to Judah

ZEBULUN THE SAILOR

'Zebulun will live by the seashore
and become a haven for ships;
his border will extend towards Sidon.'

Genesis 49:13

In this painting, Zurbarán is clearly illustrating the prophecy that Zebulun would live by the sea which is prominent in the background. Zebulun has a weathered face and a far seeing eye. He holds an oar in his left hand and an anchor in his right hand. His jaunty costume includes colourful cropped trousers that would be very acceptable on a beach today! It is thought that these materials could have come from South America. Zurbarán's studio was in Seville which was the entry point for South American goods.

There is a lightness and an optimism about this painting. Has Zurbarán chosen the anchor to represent hope? One of the possible meanings of the name Zebulun is 'wished for habitation'. Certainly the sea is often looked upon as a place of abundance with its opportunities for trade and occupations like fishing. Maybe Zurbarán is also hinting at Jesus Christ as the one who provided abundantly with the multiplication

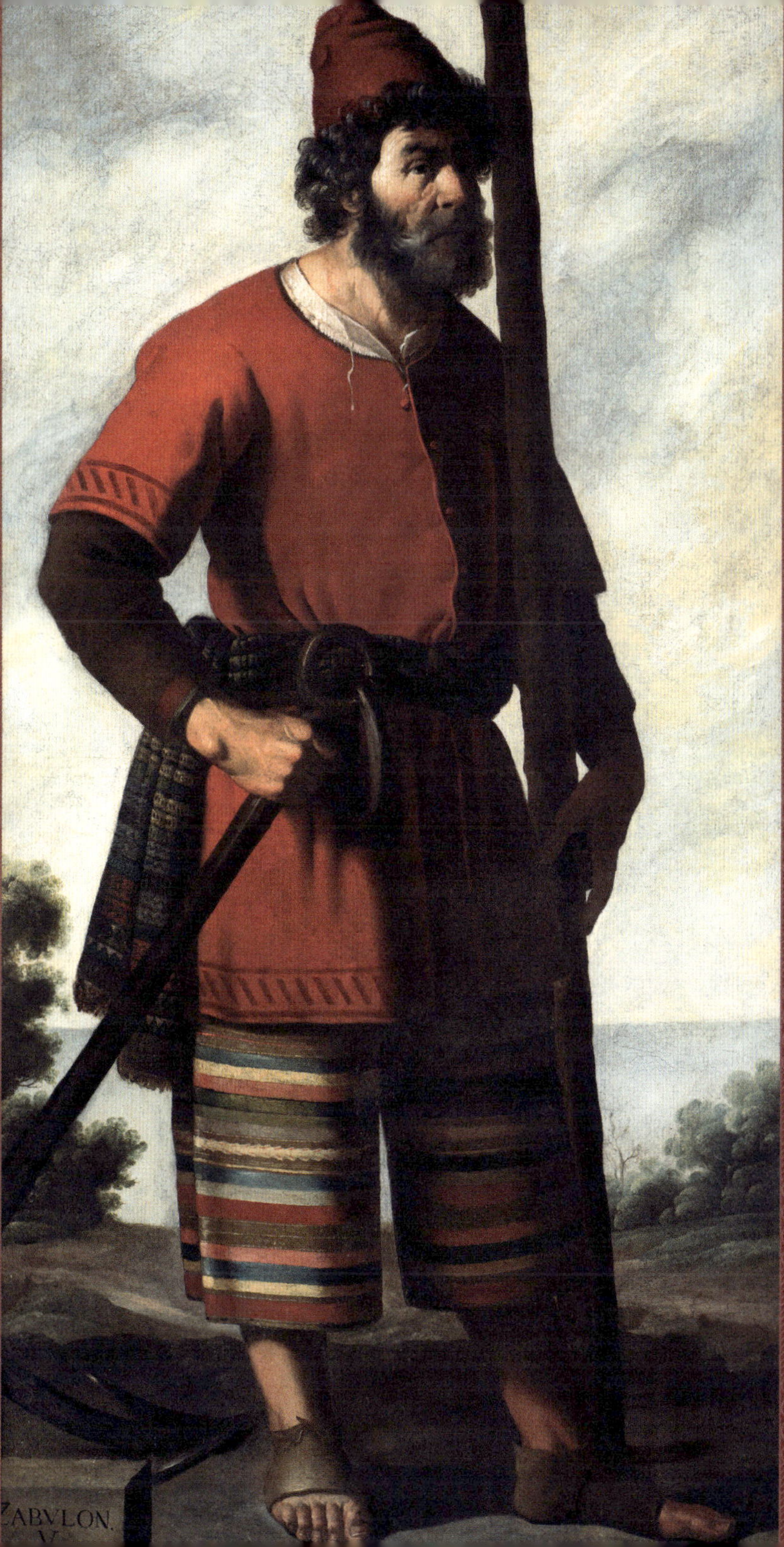
ZABVLON.
V

of fish by the Sea of Galilee and about the different kind of fishing Christ spoke of when he said, *"I will make you fishers of men"*.

As I have meditated on the paintings, I feel that Zebulun is the kind of person I'd like to get to know! He somehow communicates reliability and dependability. This is interesting because there is a reference in the Bible about men from all the different tribes coming to fight for King David and the men of Zebulun are singled out as those who came "to help David with undivided loyalty". (1 Chronicles 12:33).

Meditation Suggestions

- Where is your 'wished for habitation'? Is it your present home, a place you go to on holiday or somewhere else?
- Speaking of Christ and His work on the cross, the writer to the Hebrews says, *"We have this hope as an anchor for the soul"* (Hebrew 6:19). In early Christianity, the upturned anchor was often used as a symbol of the cross. Meditate on connections you can think of between an anchor and a cross.
- What do you hope for most?
- Can you call to mind someone who you would describe as loyal and dependable?

Listening to Zebulun

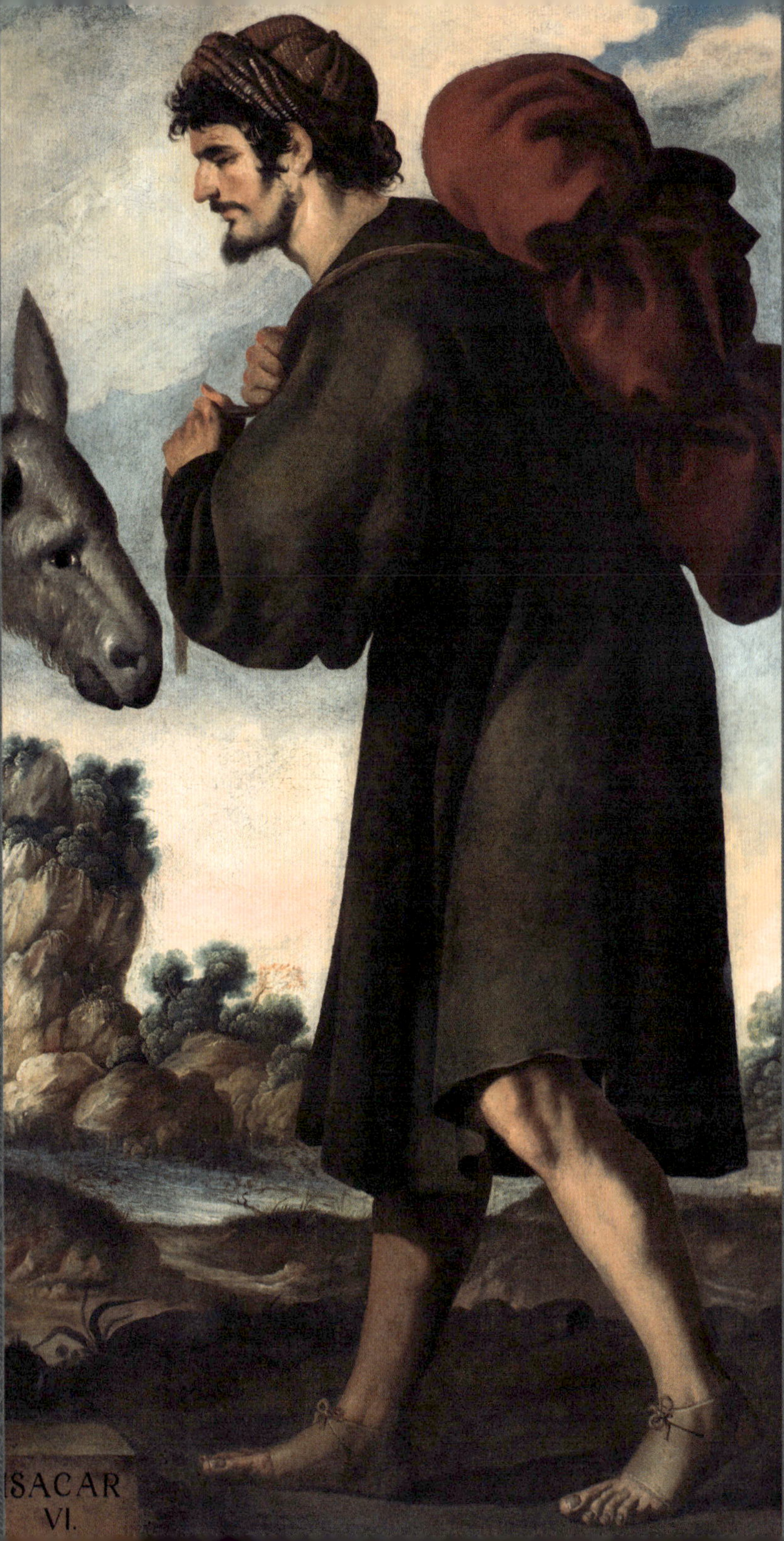
ISACAR
VI.

ISSACHER
THE BURDEN BEARER

'Issachar is a scrawny donkey
lying down among the sheepfolds.
When he sees how good is his resting place
and how pleasant is his land,
he will bend his shoulder to the burden
and submit to forced labour.

Genesis 49:14,15

So often we find that Zurbarán must have thought deeply about the Biblical text as he considered how to paint each subject. Every painting is the fruit of his meditation and this one of Issacher is no exception.

Issacher comes from a Hebrew word that, depending on its context, can mean either 'hire' or 'reward'. It is sometimes also used of a servant or hired hand. Jacob prophesied that the land that Issacher would inherit would be a good and pleasant land described as a resting place. On the other hand however, it would be a place of heavy labour. Initially, the tribe of Issacher indeed submitted to forced labour under the Canaanites, in return for being allowed to live on the land.

Eventually the land became fully theirs but, at certain times, they were again pressured into forced labour by oppressive kings like Solomon.

The donkey is known as a 'beast of burden' and is portrayed as almost in sympathy with Issacher as he carries his heavy burden on his back. Yet, in spite of the oppression, Issacher does not lose his dignity. He is strong and resilient.

Meditation Suggestions

- It is very possible that there is an allusion to Jesus Christ here. The prophet Isaiah foretold that the Messiah would be one who has *"borne our griefs and carried our sorrows"* (Isaiah 53:4). He was the suffering servant who carried out his painful task and ultimately received his reward. The posture of Issacher moving forward with his burden is reminiscent of Jesus moving forward carrying His cross. The striking red colour of the sack may be an allusion to the blood of Christ. Is that river in the background for the washing away of sins?
- Here is a quote from George Bernard Shaw to reflect on: "People become attached to their burdens sometimes more than the burdens are attached to them".

Listening to Issacher

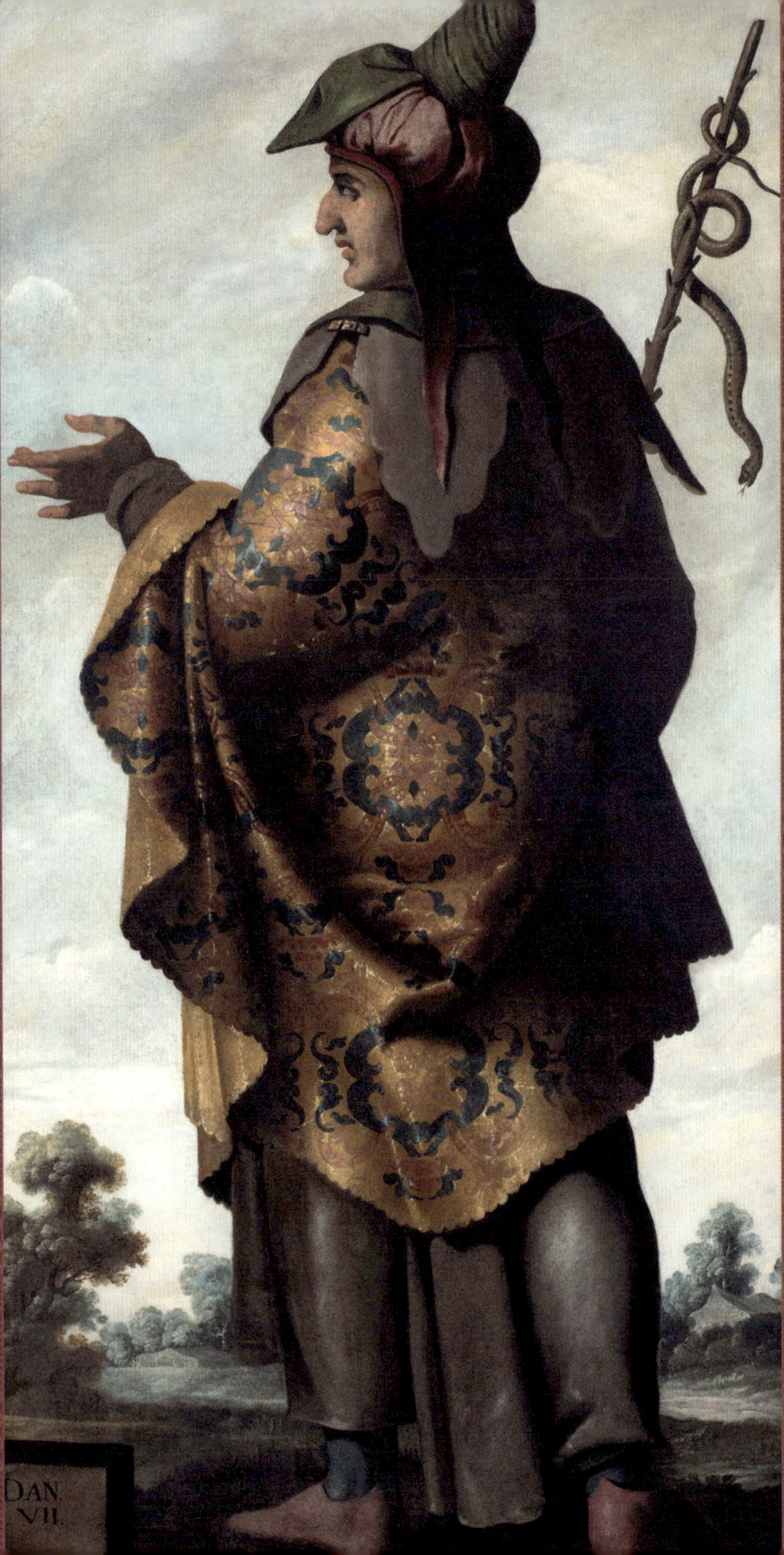
DAN.
VII.

DAN THE JUDGE

'Dan will provide justice for his people
as one of the tribes of Israel.
Dan will be a snake by the roadside,
a viper along the path,
that bites the horse's heels
so that its rider tumbles backwards.'

Genesis 49:16,17

In this very unusual portrait, Dan cuts an impressive figure in his striking headgear and gaudy cloak. He comes across as a highly intelligent man and his hand gesture suggests he is giving a judgement or dispensing advice. All this illustrates the destiny of the tribe in terms of issues of justice.

But what about the snake? Zurbarán has chosen not to paint the snake by the wayside as Jacob described it in his prophecy. Instead he has painted the snake writhing dramatically around Dan's staff. Zurbarán is a storyteller and the snake is an opportunity to reference the story recorded in Numbers 21:5-9 where, after the Israelites had been complaining, the Lord sent a plague of serpents among the people. As the snakes bit the people, they started to die and God instructed Moses to make a bronze serpent on a pole. Whoever looked on the serpent would live. This is the origin of the snake on the pole as a symbol of healing. In John's gospel the snake on the pole is likened to Christ on the cross: "Just as Moses lifted up the snake in the wilderness, so the Son of Man must be lifted up, that everyone who believes may have eternal life". (John 3:14,15).

Meditation Suggestions

- Is there an issue of justice you are facing in your circumstances now? What advice might you imagine Dan passing on to you?
- Justice and healing are often closely linked. Think about situations you know about, where restorative rather than retributive justice might be used.
- Take the opportunity to meditate on the snake on the pole and to compare it with the cross of Christ. What do these symbols mean to you?

Listening to Dan

GAD
THE SOLDIER

'I look for your deliverance, Lord.'
'Gad will be attacked by a band of raiders,
but he will attack them at their heels.' Genesis 49:18,19

The first sentence "I look for your deliverance, O Lord" is most probably a brief prayer from Jacob, asking for God's help as he continues the prophecies. Perhaps also he is thinking about deliverance through his impending death to the after life. However it fits well also with Jacob's prophecy for Gad. That simple prayer may well have been passed on by Gad to his descendants in the context of their destiny as a distinctly military tribe.

Gad was the son of Zilpah, Leah's servant girl. Because of this, he could have felt inferior to his brothers, but the indications are that he grew up to be self-assertive and bold. His name means good fortune, but it is the kind of good fortune that is gained through struggle.

Zurbarán paints him as a soldier with his breastplate, his huge sword and his mighty club. He looks out confidently ready to shake your hand and it would be a very firm handshake

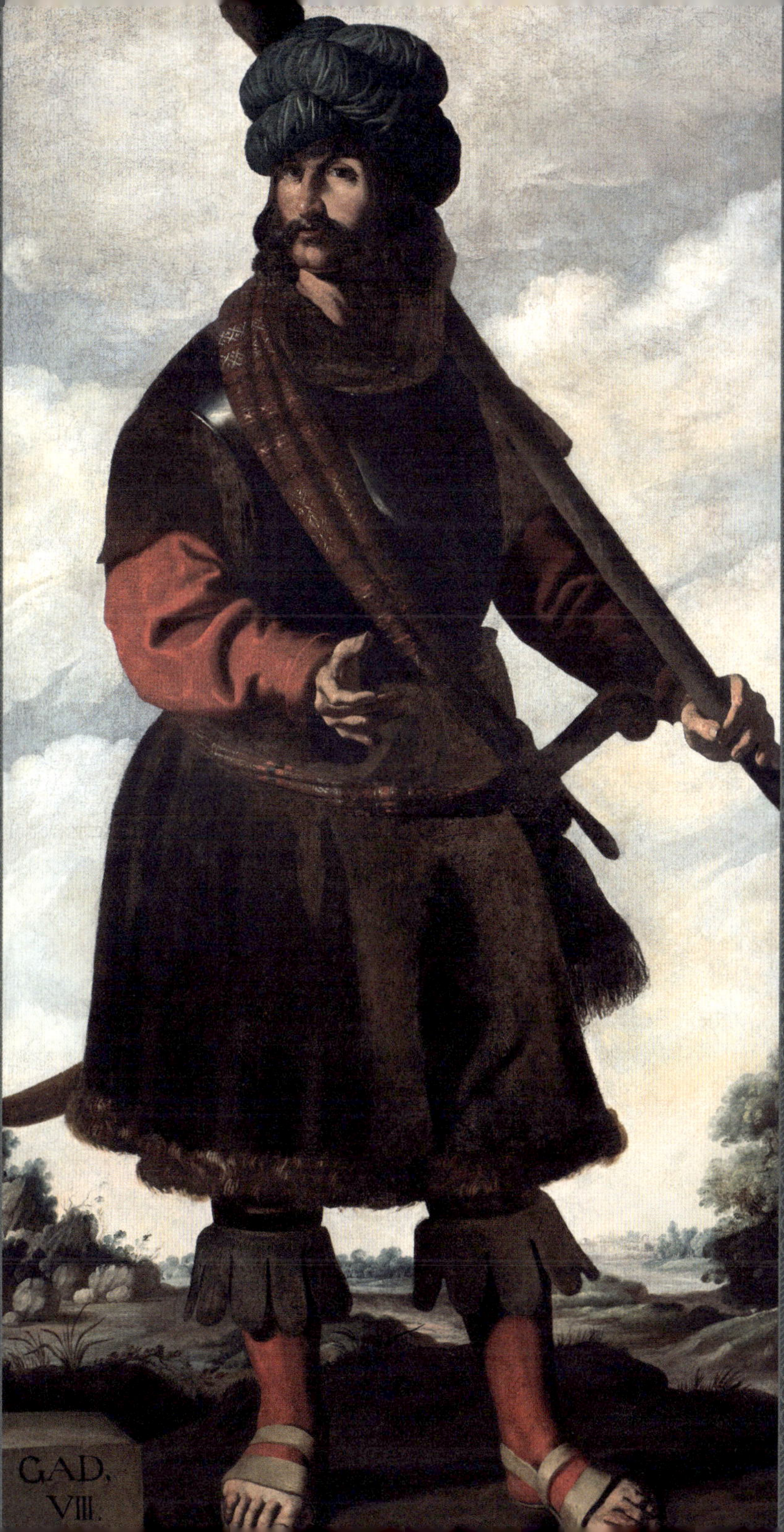
GAD,
VIII.

indeed! According to rabbinical literature, Jacob did not present Gad to Pharaoh along with his other sons. Because Gad was so obviously a warrior, Jacob feared that Pharaoh would notice and conscript him for his royal bodyguard!

Gad was ready for adversity and accepted it as part of his destiny, but he was also confident that he would overcome. It is interesting that when they came to the Promised Land, the tribe of Gad voluntarily chose to have their land on the east side of the Jordan in the area most exposed to enemies.

Meditation Suggestions

- In the New Testament, the image of the soldier and of weapons is transformed into that of overcoming the powers of evil. Here are some phrases from St Paul's letter to the Ephesians to meditate on: *"Be strong in the Lord and in his mighty power. Put on the full armour of God, so that you can take your stand against the devil's schemes. For our struggle is not against flesh and blood, but against the rulers, against the authorities, against the powers of this dark world and against the spiritual forces of evil in the heavenly realms. Therefore put on the full armour of God, so that when the day of evil comes, you may be able to stand your ground, and after you have done everything, to stand. Stand firm then, with the belt of truth buckled around your waist, with the breastplate of righteousness in place, and with your feet fitted with the readiness that comes from the gospel of peace... Take the sword of the Spirit which is the word of God".* (Ephesians 6:10-17)

Listening to Gad

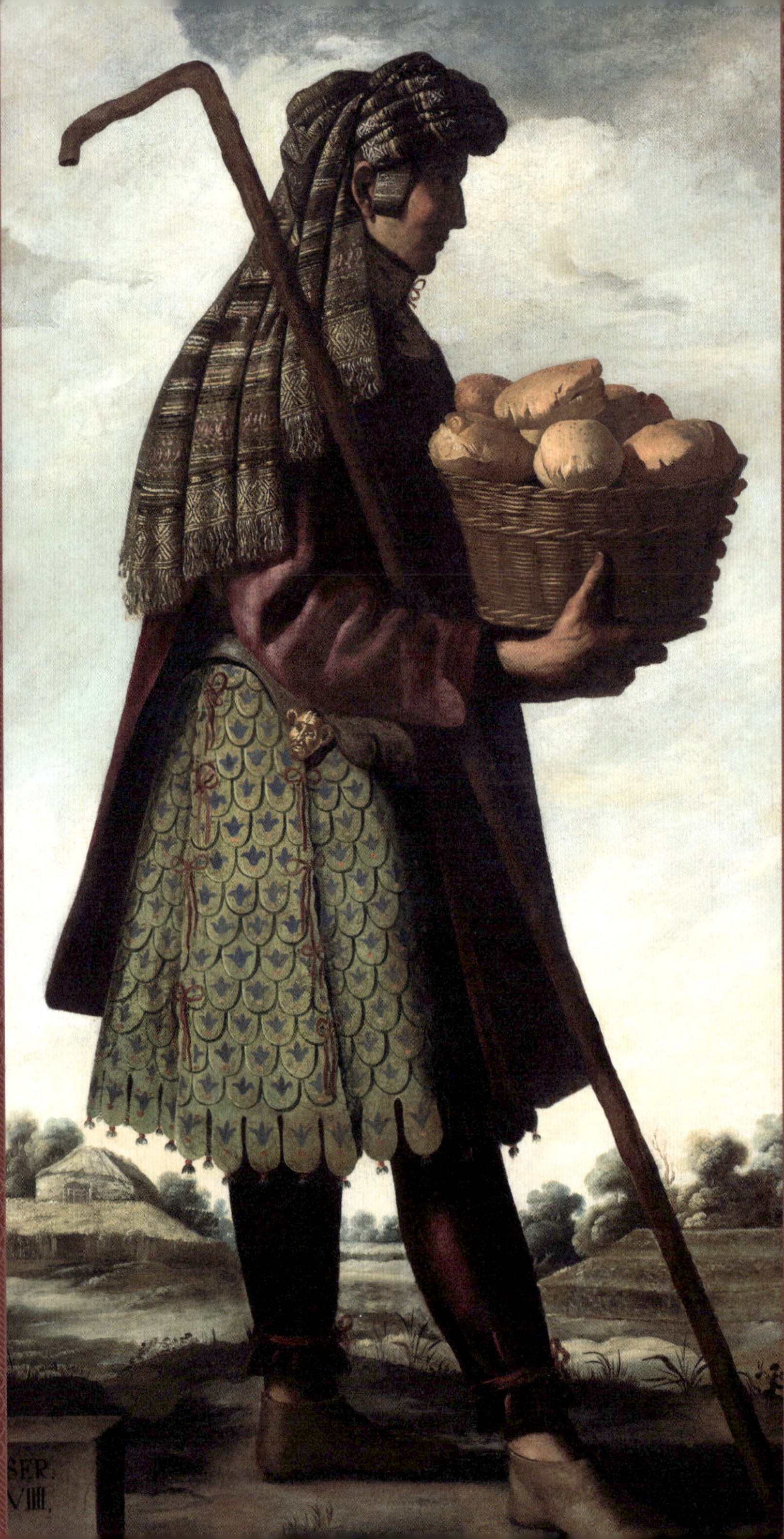
SER.
VIIII,

ASHER
THE JOY BRINGER

'Asher's food will be rich;
he will provide delicacies fit for a king.' Genesis 49:20

Asher's name means happy and later the tribe of Asher gained a reputation as the happy tribe. As Jacob's brief prophecy suggests, a major reason for that happiness was that Asher lived in the fertile coastal area of north west Israel. The area was well known as the best place for growing olives which are also a symbol of joy.

Asher is portrayed as a farmer with cornfields in the landscape behind him, but he is clearly not in his working clothes! He is dressed in such fine clothes because he is on his way to present his delicacies to the king. And what fine delicacies they are! The basket with the loaves of bread is like a painting within a painting. Zurbarán was a master of still life painting.

Living in Seville, Zurbarán was likely to be familiar with the great sixth century theologian Isidore of Seville. Isidore taught that because of his association with bread, Asher was a type of Christ. Zurbarán is reminding us of Christ's giving of the bread to the thousands by the Sea of Galilee, to the disciples at the Last Supper and again to the disciples by the Sea of Galilee after his resurrection.

As if to underscore the fact that Asher is a type of Christ, Zurbarán also gives Asher a shepherd's crook to remind us of Jesus as the Good Shepherd.

And what about that curious grotesque gold mask that Asher wears by his right elbow? Is it in that central position to suggest that Asher is pure gold or is it there just to make you smile - after all Asher, like Jesus, was a joy bringer! The fact that Asher seems to also have two left feet is perhaps something else especially designed to amuse!

Meditation Suggestions

- This painting is full of joy. What aspects of it particularly delight you?
- Jesus described himself as "the bread of life". Focus on the basket of bread and meditate on that phrase. Is there something here to feed your soul?
- What might it mean for us today to "provide delicacies for for a king"? Reflect on these phrases from the parable of the sheep and the goats: *"Then the King will say to those on his right, 'Come, you who are blessed by my Father; take your inheritance, the kingdom prepared for you since the creation of the world. For I was hungry and you gave me something to eat...' "Then the righteous will answer him, 'Lord, when did we see you hungry and feed you?...' "The King will reply, 'Truly I tell you, whatever you did for one of the least of these brothers and sisters of mine, you did for me.'*

Listening to Asher

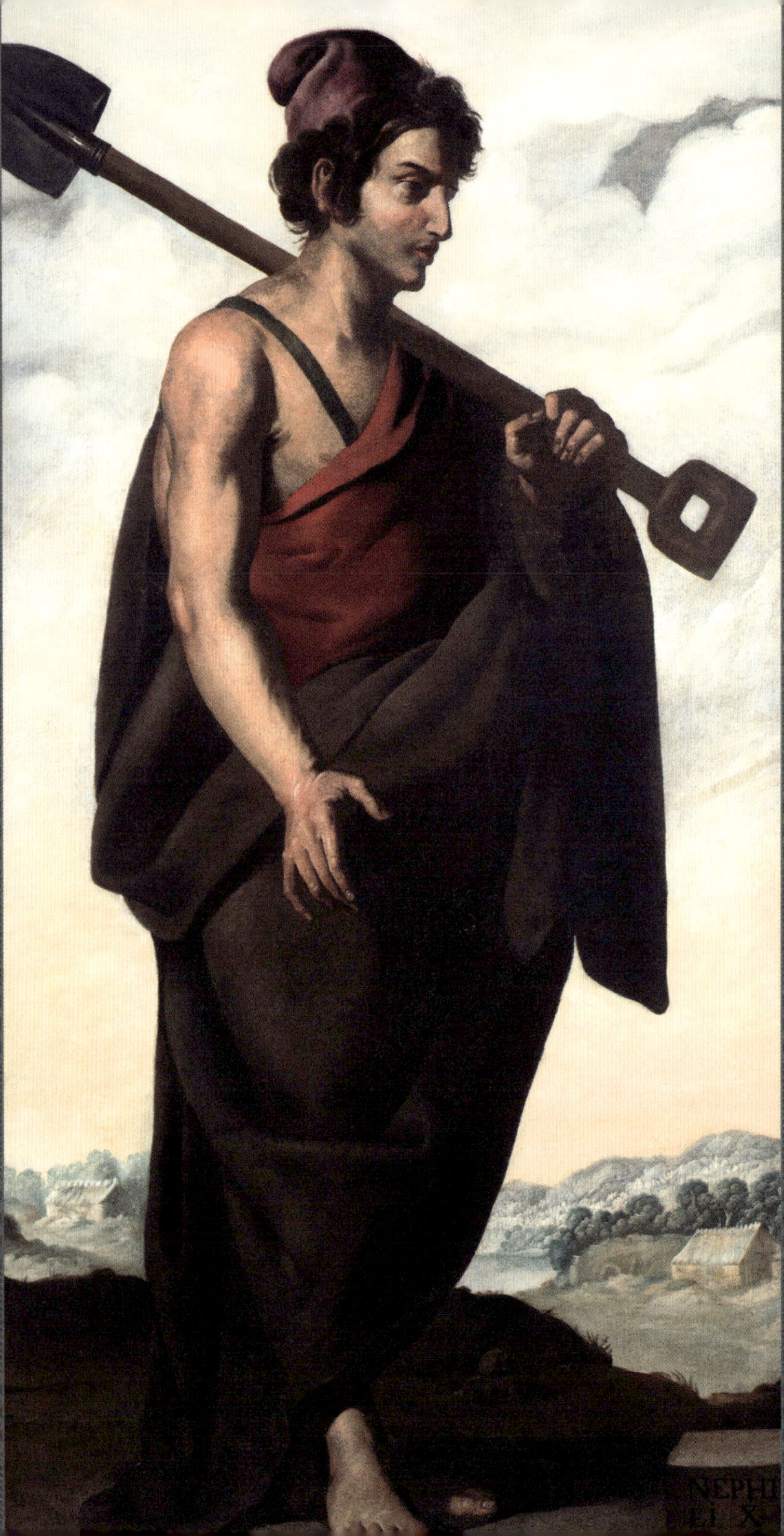

NAPHTALI THE GARDENER

'Naphtali is a doe set free
he gives beautiful words.' Genesis 49:21

When Zurbarán painted Naphtali, he did not include any direct reference to the deer in Jacob's prophecy, but he does portray him as a lithe and very healthy looking young man. According to Jewish tradition, Naphtali was a very good runner!

There is also a strong physical element in the meaning of his name which is wrestler. Interestingly it was the mothers Leah and Rachel who named the boys rather than Jacob himself, but this name would have meant much to Jacob who had a memorable wrestling match with God recorded in Genesis 32:22-32.

As is so often the case with this series of paintings, it seems that Zurbarán is wanting to tell us another story and to point us to Jesus Christ. His posture for Naphtali is clearly a borrowing from a print by Albrecht Dürer of Christ appearing to Mary Magdalene at his resurrection. There we see the exposed limb and the shovel over the shoulder. Mary had thought that Jesus was the gardener, but when he spoke the word "Mary" she soon recognised him. It is interesting to reflect that, if indeed Zurbarán is suggesting an image of Christ, it is probably much closer to what Jesus may have looked like as a dark haired young Jew, than the older Germanic Jesus of Dürer!

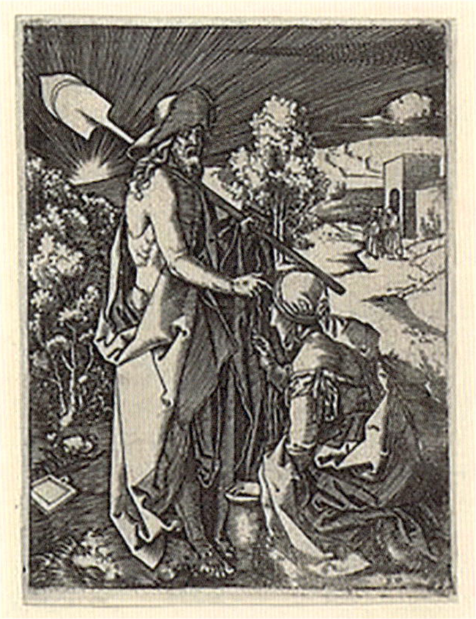

Zurbarán has given Naphtali an open kindly face and again this reinforces the sense of prefiguring Christ. In the second part of Jacob's prophecy, which is difficult to translate from the Hebrew, one rendering is about eloquent speech which is a reminder that people "were amazed at the gracious words that came out of his [Jesus'] lips". (Luke 4:22)

Meditation Suggestions

- How do you imagine the face of Christ? Has your image of him changed over the years?
- "He gives beautiful words". Mary Magdalene would surely have said that Jesus spoke beautiful words to her, bringing healing and transformation. Is there anyone you could pass on words of encouragement to at this time?

Listening to Naphtali

JOSEPH THE BLESSED

'Joseph is a fruitful vine, a fruitful vine near a spring, whose branches climb over a wall.
With bitterness archers attacked him; they shot at him with hostility.
But his bow remained steady, his strong arms stayed supple, because of the hand of the Mighty One of Jacob, because of the Shepherd, the Rock of Israel, because of your father's God, who helps you, because of the Almighty, who blesses you with blessings of the skies above, blessings of the deep springs below, blessings of the breast and womb.
Your father's blessings are greater than the blessings of the ancient mountains, than the bounty of the age-old hills.
Let all these rest on the head of Joseph, on the brow of the prince among his brothers.'

Genesis 49:22-26

In Jacob's prophecy for Joseph, we can truly say that this is an uninterrupted blessing - indeed the word blessing occurs six times and is found nowhere else in the prophecies. Joseph's name means 'he adds' and certainly Jacob added one blessing after another upon Joseph. It is no wonder

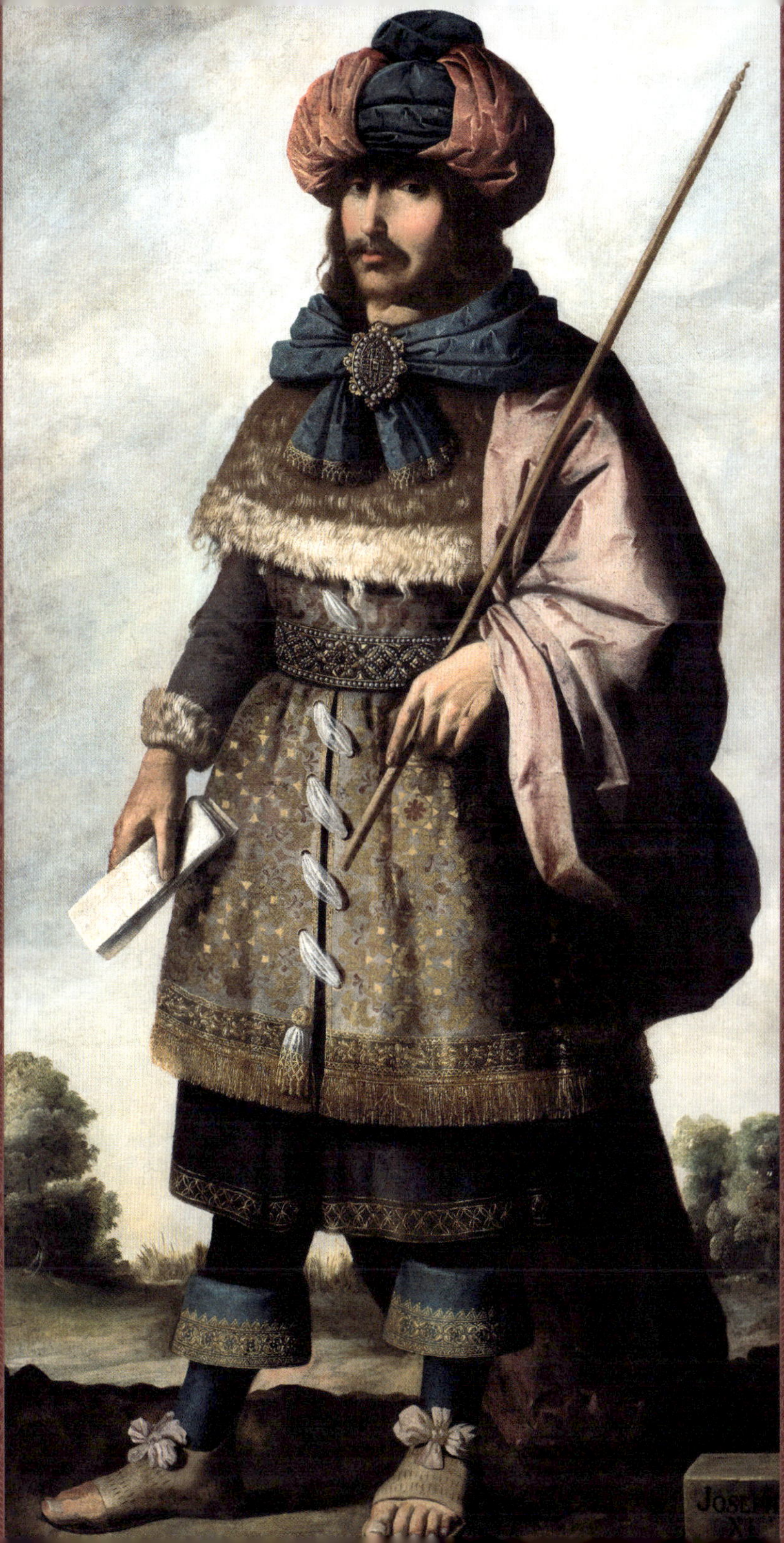

then that Zurbarán painted Joseph as a supremely blessed individual. He stands confidently, calmly and at ease. He is dressed in all his finery as the Viceroy of Egypt, although his costume reminds us more of Moorish fashions, which would have been more familiar to Zurbarán than Egyptian clothing. Every item of his clothing from his turban to his sandals with bows is meticulously painted. In his left hand, Joseph carries a rod of office and in his right he holds a document - perhaps the authorisation for his position from the Pharaoh himself.

Of all the brothers, Joseph is the one who is most frequently mentioned as a type of Christ. Like Jesus, Joseph was the beloved son of his father, he went to Egypt and he was falsely accused and condemned. Joseph was 'the saviour of the world' at that time and he forgave his brothers as Jesus forgave those who crucified him. It would be surprising if this was not on Zurbarán's mind as he planned this portrait. Perhaps it is a deliberate contrast to the Christ type portrayed in the previous painting of Naphtali. Here is an image that prefigures Christ as the sovereign Lord and the just and compassionate Prince of Peace.

Meditation Suggestions

- Refer back to Griffin Oleyneck's meditation on page 23. What do you see and hear from Joseph?

Listening to Joseph

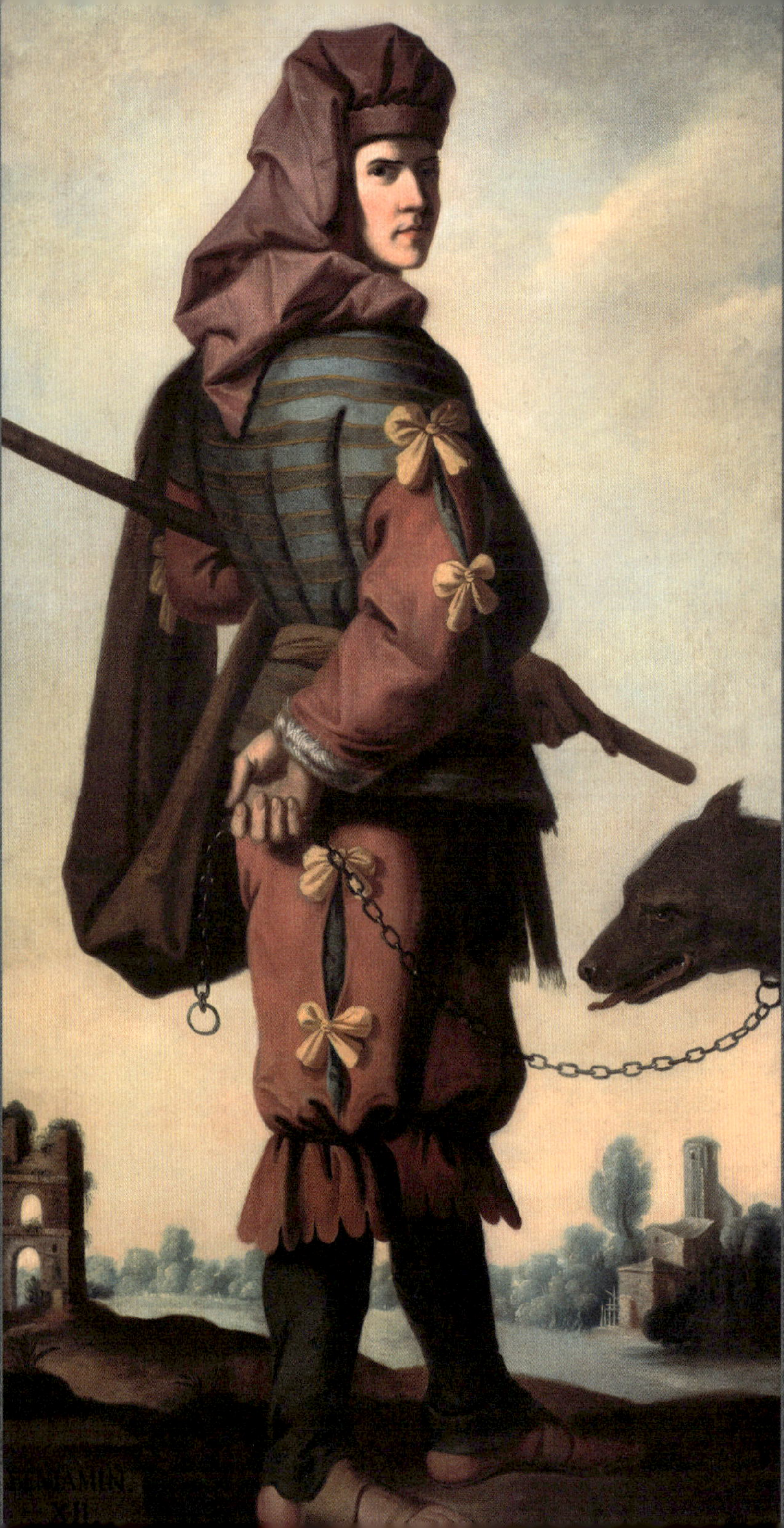

BENJAMIN
THE FAVOURED SON

'Benjamin is a ravenous wolf;
in the morning he devours the prey,
in the evening he divides the plunder.' Genesis 49:27

Like Joseph, Benjamin was another favourite son and his name means 'son of my right hand.' This implied that he was very dear to Jacob and the right hand is often about blessing. However there is not much blessing in evidence here and, as with most of the other sons, Jacob is prophesying the destiny of both Benjamin and the tribe rather than blessing him.

The prophecy of Jacob describing Benjamin as a ravenous wolf was certainly fulfilled in the history of the tribe. The tribe soon gained a reputation for producing formidable warriors who were particularly skilled as archers and slingers. They were also trained to be ambidextrous. The tribe was almost wiped out in the Battle of Gibeah and after that time they remained a small tribe, but continued their reputation as ferocious fighters. The first Israelite king, Saul, was from the tribe of Benjamin as was the apostle Paul. When we first hear about Paul, he is very much like a ravenous wolf with his murderous campaign against the followers of Jesus. After his dramatic encounter with Christ, Paul conducted a very different campaign declaring that "we do not fight against flesh and blood but against principalities, against powers of this dark world" (Ephesians 6:12) and at the end of his life he could say, "I have fought a good fight, I have finished my course, I have kept the faith". (2 Timothy 4:7)

In his portrait of Benjamin, Zurbarán shows him twisting round to look out from the canvas. He holds the rather doggy wolf by a chain. In the background Zurbarán includes the temple. Jerusalem was partly in the territory of Benjamin and some old Jewish interpretations of the ravenous wolf explain that it refers to the way the ravenous fire on the altar consumed the animal sacrifices. Another feature is that Zurbarán has Benjamin carrying a bag which is a reminder of the story in Genesis 44 where Joseph's cup was hidden in Benjamin's bag.

In most of Zurbarán's portraits in this series there is some connection with Jesus Christ. In the print on the following page by Albrecht Dürer of Christ being nailed to the cross, Zurbarán has directly borrowed the posture of Benjamin and elements of his clothing from the figure on the left. Two incidents in the life of St Paul come to mind. Firstly, when he stood by while Stephen was stoned to death, and secondly, when on the road to Damascus, Jesus asked him the question, "Why are you persecuting me?". Perhaps a message of the painting is that those, like St Paul, who follow the way of the ravenous wolf, will ultimately have to come face to face with the crucified and risen Christ. Perhaps transformation is suggested in this painting - Benjamin looks relaxed, the chain is held loosely and maybe that ravenous wolf is turning into a friendly tame dog!

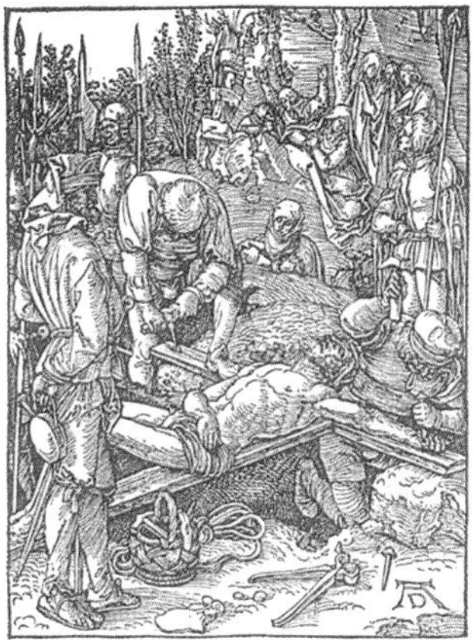

Meditation Suggestions

- Would you say that you have had any experience of transformation in your life?
- As you come to this last painting in the series, are you left with any overall impressions or specific things you have seen and heard and which need further meditation or action?

Listening to Benjamin

POSTSCRIPT

As I have been writing these meditations, I have sometimes wondered what Zurbarán himself would make of them. I suspect that occasionally, he might say, “Yes, that is what I had in mind”. More often I think he would say, “No, I certainly wasn’t thinking about that at all!” He might also sometimes say, “How on earth did you miss that message?” However, I suspect that Zurbarán would also have no problems with, for example, the idea of Issacher foreshadowing Christ as the burden bearer, even if he had not intended that. As we have seen when considering the painting of Zurbarán at the foot of the cross on page 21, he is sometimes consciously pointing to Christ or to some other Christian truth, but because he would have believed in the guidance and inspiration of the Holy Spirit in his art, he would be content with recognising that mysteries can be revealed through the unconscious mind as well.

I hope you have found this meditational guide helpful and enriching. I am sure there is much more to be gleaned from these paintings, so if you would like to share any insights that you have gained, please contact me at dlpott@gmail.com

IMAGE CREDITS

Page 7
Francisco José de Goya y Lucientes (1746-1828)
Portrait of Francisco de Zurbarán (1598-1664) C 1798
Sanguine on white paper, 15.1 x 11 cm
Paris, Louvre museum, D.A.G.
Photo © RMN-Grand Palais (Louvre museum) /
Michèle Bellot

Portrait intended to illustrate the *Diccionario historico de los mas ilustres professores de Bellas Artes de las bellas artes de Espana* by Juan Agustin Cean Bermudez, published in 1800 in Madrid on the initiative of the Academia de San Fernando.

Page 8
Francisco de Zurbarán (1598-1664)
Agnus Dei, 1635-1640
Oil on canvas, 38 x 62 cm
Photo © Museo Nacional del Prado

Page 9
Francisco de Zurbarán (1598-1664)
Portrait of King Philip IV of Spain, Before 1650
Oil on canvas, 35 x 28 cm
Slovak National Museum - Betliar Museum, Betliar manor-house, from the collection of Andrássy family
Photo Vlado Eliáš

Page 10
Circle of Francisco de Zurbarán Spanish, (1598-1664)
Abigail, 17th century
Oil on canvas, 70 ½ x 41 1/4 in, SN342
Bequest of John Ringling, 1936 Collection of The John and Mable Ringling
Photo Museum of Art, the State Art Museum of Florida

Page 13
Vox Populi Vox Dei or the Jew Act Repealed, 1753
Etching and engraving
CC licensed attribution - CC BY-NC-SA 4.0

Page 14
Thomas Hudson (1701-1779)
Richard Trevor, Bishop of Durham, 1756
Oil on canvas, 49 x 39 in
Photo Courtesy of The Auckland Project / The Church Commissioners

Page 15
Jacob Jordaens (1593-1678)
The Four Fathers of the Latin Church C 1650
Oil on canvas, 209 x 252 cm
Photo Courtesy of The Auckland Project

Page 19
Photo: House of Hues
Photo Courtesy of The Auckland Project

Page 21
Francisco de Zurbarán (1598-1664)
The Crucified Christ with a Painter, C 1650
Oil on canvas, 105 x 84 cm
Photo © Museo Nacional del Prado

Pages 24-69

Francisco de Zurbarán (1598-1664)

Jacob and his Twelve Sons 1640-1645

Oil on canvas

All paintings are between 199.4 to 201.3 cm high and 102.4 to 104 cm wide

Photos: Justin Piperger

Photo Courtesy of The Auckland Project

Page 66

Albrecht Dürer (1471–1528)

Christ Appearing to Mary Magdalene, from The Small Passion c 1510

Woodcut, 12.7 x 9.8 cm

Photo The Metropolitan Museum of Art, New York

Page 72

Arthur Pond (C 1705-1758)

After Francisco de Zurbarán

Benjamin 1756

Oil on canvas, 198 x 102 cm

Photo: Justin Piperger

Photo Courtesy of The Auckland Project

This painting is a copy of the original painting by Zurbarán which hangs in Grimsthorpe Castle, Lincolnshire.

Page 75

Albrecht Dürer (1471–1528)

Christ Nailed to the Cross, from The Small Passion c 1509

Woodcut, 12.7 x 9.8 cm

Photo The Metropolitan Museum of Art, New York